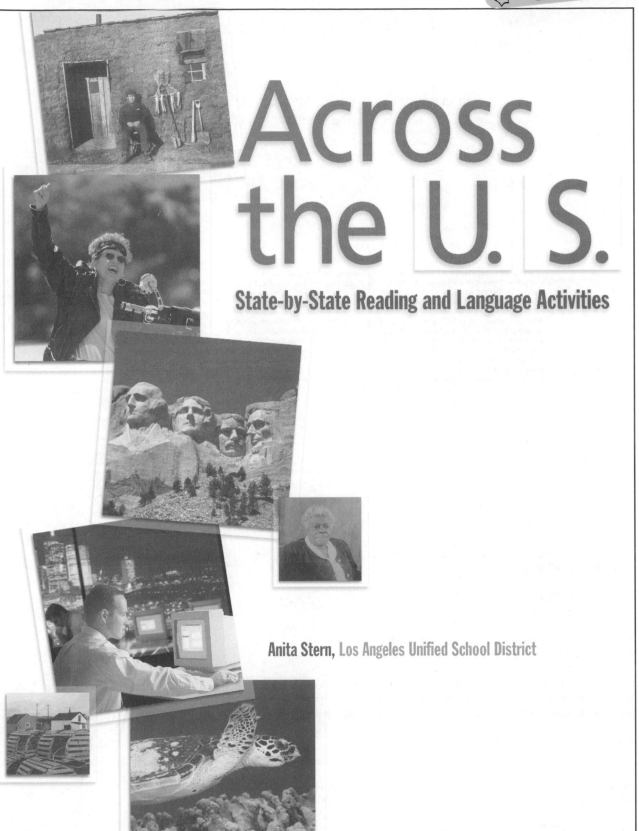

Across the U. S.

State-by-State Reading and Language Activities

Anita Stern, Los Angeles Unified School District

New Readers Press

In memory of my uncle, Abraham Itzchak Goodman.
His flame went out too soon.

Cover photos courtesy of: Hulton Archive/Getty Images; Creatas/DigitalVision; © Glen Allison/PhotoDisc/PictureQuest; Library of Congress, Prints & Photographs Division, Carl Van Vechten Collection, LC-USZ62-42476 DLC; © PhotoLink/PhotoDisc/PictureQuest; Ken Usami/PhotoDisc/PictureQuest; DigitalVision/PictureQuest; www.comstock.com; Library of Congress, Prints and Photographs Division, Detroit Publishing Company Collection; © Corbis Images/PictureQuest

Photos courtesy of: p. 6 Sikorsky Image Gallery; p. 9 © PhotoLink/PhotoDisc/PictureQuest; p.12, 97, 134 www.comstock.com; p. 18 Library of Congress; p. 25 Lewes Historical Society; p. 28 DigitalVision/PictureQuest; p. 31, 50 Getty Images/DigitalVision; p. 34, 84 Library of Congress, Prints and Photographs Division, Detroit Publishing Company Collection; p. 37 Library of Congress, Prints and Photographs Division LC-USZ62-117116 DLC; p. 40 Library of Congress, Prints and Photographs Division, Historic American Buildings Survey or Historic American Engineering Record HABS, WVA, 19 HARF,2-4; p. 44 USDA History Collection, Special Collections, National Agricultural Library; p 47 © Tomi/PhotoLink/PhotoDisc/PictureQuest; p. 56 Getty Images/EyeWire; p. 68 Library of Congress, Prints & Photographs Division, Carl Van Vechten Collection, LC-USZ62-42476 DLC; p. 75 Artemis Images/Indianapolis Motor Speedway; p. 78 Library of Congress, Prints and Photographs Division, Historic American Buildings Survey or Historic American Engineering Record, HAER, NY,31-NEYO,89-11; p. 91 Sever's Corn Maze & Fall Festival; p. 100 Library of Congress, Prints & Photographs Division, FSA-OWI Collection, LC-USW3-030283-D DLC; p. 103 Creatas/DigitalVision; p. 107 © Corbis Images/PictureQuest; p 125 PhotoLink/PhotoDisc/PictureQuest; p. 128 © Glen Allison/PhotoDisc/PictureQuest; p. 138 Library of Congress, Prints and Photographs Division; p. 141, 147 Western History/Genealogy Department, Denver Public Library; p. 144 Woolaroc Museum; p. 154 Ken Usami/PhotoDisc/PictureQuest; p. 167 National Library of Medicine

Across the U.S. Student Book
State-by-State Readings and Language Activities
ISBN 1-56420-293-3

Copyright © 2004 New Readers Press
New Readers Press
Division of ProLiteracy Worldwide
1320 Jamesville Avenue, Syracuse, New York 13210
www.newreaderspress.com

Printed in the United States of America
9 8 7 6 5 4 3 2 1

All proceeds from the sale of New Readers Press materials
support literacy programs in the United States and worldwide.

Acquisitions Editor: Paula L. Schlusberg
Content Editor: Judi Lauber
Production Director: Heather Witt-Badoud
Designer: Kimbrly Koennecke
Illustrations: Luciana Mallozzi, Linda Tiff
Cover Design: Andrea Woodbury

Contents

Contents

Northeast Region

Connecticut, Maine, Massachusetts, New Hampshire, Rhode Island, Vermont

A Quick Look at this Region

Early in the history of the United States, small ships anchored on the rocky northern coast of North America. Many of the first European colonists settled there. The land between Long Island and Nova Scotia was named New England.

In early colonial days, the 1600s, many of America's best-known writers were New Englanders. In the 1700s, New England was important in the struggle for independence from Great Britain. After the American Revolution, the region became the young nation's first center of industry. Cloth making was especially important there. In the 1800s, many abolitionist leaders came from New England. These people struggled to end slavery in the United States.

Today, New England is known for fine universities, medical centers, and high-tech computer engineering. Thousands of people visit every year to see New England's historic sites. These sites show what life was like in the early days of our nation.

Connecticut

Thinking about the Picture

1. Who is using this helicopter? How might they use it?
2. What are some other uses of helicopters?
3. How is a helicopter different from an airplane?

Helicopters

 Helicopters are different from other aircraft, and they have many uses. The first practical helicopter was made in Connecticut. Today, countries around the world use helicopters from the state.

Helicopters have rotors on top that go round and round quickly. The movement lifts the helicopter into the air and lets it fly many ways. A helicopter can move forward, backward, sideways, or straight up and down. It can stay in the air at one point. It can take off and land on a small space. It can fly lower and slower than an airplane, but it cannot fly as fast. It needs more fuel than an airplane, so it is more expensive to fly.

Igor Sikorsky, a Russian immigrant, built and flew the first practical helicopter in 1939. He ran an airplane company in Stratford, Connecticut. Sikorsky Aircraft is still there today.

Sikorsky improved his early helicopters, and in 1942, the U.S. government ordered them for the first time. Britain and the United States used helicopters in World War II. The U.S. also used helicopters during the Korean War and the Vietnam War. They rescued soldiers, carried the wounded, and were used in battle. Sikorsky helicopters are still used.

Helicopters also have many peacetime uses. In 1945, for the first time, a helicopter made a rescue at sea. They save lives every year by lifting people from canyons, mountains, car accidents, burning buildings, and sinking ships. They bring food and medicine to places airplanes cannot reach because of floods, earthquakes, and storms.

Radio and TV stations use helicopters to watch traffic. Police use them to follow suspects, and farmers use them to drop seeds and fertilizer on their fields. Firefighters drop water from helicopters onto forest fires. In all, more than 40 countries use helicopters made in Connecticut.

A First Look at Vocabulary

Match each term with its meaning.

_____ **1.** aircraft   a. going down under water

_____ **2.** branches   b. save

_____ **3.** expensive   c. the number and movement of automobiles

_____ **4.** flood   d. water covering land that is usually dry

_____ **5.** fuel   e. parts of a machine that go around

_____ **6.** rescue   f. divisions or parts of something larger

_____ **7.** rotors   g. costly; high-priced

_____ **8.** sinking   h. machine that flies

_____ **9.** take off   i. material that burns to supply power

_____ **10.** traffic   j. lift from the ground and begin to fly

A Second Look at Vocabulary

Complete the story. Use the words from the first exercise.

Helicopters are a kind of _____ that can fly backward, sideways,
[1]
up, and down. They can _____ from small places because they can
[2]
fly straight up. They have _____ on top that go around quickly and
[3]
make them fly. Helicopters need more power than airplanes do, so they burn more

_____. This makes them more _____ to use than
[4]   [5]
airplanes are. They also do some jobs that airplanes cannot.

The Army, Navy, and other _____ of the U.S. armed forces use
[6]
helicopters. They use them for carrying troops, medicine, and supplies, and in battle.

Helicopters have many peacetime uses, too. Helicopters _____
[7]
people who are in danger. For example, they save people from

_____ ships. Sometimes a river gets too big after heavy rains, and
[8]
helicopters save people from the _____. People use helicopters to
[9]
watch _____ so other people can travel the roads more safely.
[10]

Connecticut

Understanding the Reading

Choose the best answer.

_____ 1. Helicopters are like airplanes *except*
    a. they need fuel to fly.
    b. they can take off from the ground.
    c. they can fly backward and sideways.

_____ 2. Sikorsky was a Russian immigrant who
    a. built the first practical helicopter.
    b. refused to sell helicopters to the U.S. armed forces.
    c. built fast helicopters.

_____ 3. Farmers use helicopters to
    a. pick fruit.
    b. drop seeds and fertilizer.
    c. water their fields.

Reading between the Lines

Look carefully at the reading. Mark each statement *T* for *true* or *F* for *false*.

_____ 1. Helicopters take the place of airplanes.

_____ 2. Igor Sikorsky helped build the aircraft industry in the United States.

_____ 3. Helicopters are a fast, cheap way to travel from city to city.

_____ 4. Igor Sikorsky built helicopters before he built airplanes.

Fact or Opinion?

Mark each statement *F* for *fact* or *O* for *opinion*.

_____ 1. Sikorsky helicopters are the best helicopters in the world.

_____ 2. There are many uses for helicopters.

_____ 3. The U.S. armed forces spend millions of dollars on helicopters.

_____ 4. Helicopters are less useful during peace than during war.

What Do You Think?
Discuss these questions.

1. Would you like to fly in a helicopter? Explain.
2. Is the company Sikorsky Aircraft important to Connecticut? Why or why not?

A Last Look
Write about one of these topics.

1. Look up helicopters. What are the different kinds of helicopters? What are some special uses of each kind?
2. Sikorsky was a Russian immigrant to the United States. How did he help this country? How do other immigrants help this country?
3. What kinds of work have you seen helicopters do? How would people do these jobs without helicopters?

Maine

Thinking about the Picture

1. Describe these lobster traps. What are they made of?
2. How are lobsters caught? Where?
3. What do these traps tell you about the lobster industry?

The Lobster and Fishing Industry

Maine has more than 2,500 lakes and ponds and 5,000 streams. It also has more than 200 miles of coastline on the Atlantic Ocean. As a result, the state is famous for its fishing industry.

As early as 1623, colonial fishermen were catching cod in Maine's coastal waters. Today the fishing industry is still key in the state's economy. Maine fishermen catch more than $250 million worth of fish and shellfish each year. Maine sells fresh, frozen, and canned fish in the United States and overseas.

Maine is especially famous for lobsters. It produces more lobsters than any other state. Today, lobster is a costly food, but that was not always true. In colonial times, only children, prisoners, and servants ate it. Lobsters were also used as fertilizer for crops. But around 1810, fishermen began to sell lobsters as a luxury food. The lobster fishing industry developed by about 1840.

Lobsters live on the ocean floor. Hard, jointed shells protect their bodies. Each lobster has two large claws and eight walking legs. If a lobster loses a claw or leg, it can grow it again. The claws help a lobster catch and eat food. Fishermen trap lobsters in cages called "pots," using dead fish as bait. They lower the lobster pots to the ocean floor, tying a float to each one so that they can find it again. Lobsters enter the cages to eat the fish and cannot get out again.

Today Maine fishermen catch millions of lobsters every year in the cold Atlantic waters. Restaurants in coastal towns specialize in lobster dishes. Because lobster meat spoils quickly, cooks usually boil lobsters alive. When a lobster is alive, the shell is usually greenish-black with touches of red or orange. When a lobster is cooked, the shell turns red.

A First Look at Vocabulary

Choose the best definition for each word in bold type.

_____ 1. Maine's **coastline** is on the Atlantic Ocean.
   a. area with water   b. land next to the sea   c. dry land

_____ 2. Fishing is important to Maine's **economy.**
   a. system of earning money   b. way of fishing   c. type of food

_____ 3. Today, lobster is a **luxury** food.
   a. expensive   b. popular   c. delicious

_____ 4. A lobster has a **shell** and eight legs.
   a. back   b. head   c. hard covering

_____ 5. Lobsters have two large **claws.**
   a. walking legs   b. scissor-like feet   c. feelers

_____ 6. Fishermen **trap** lobsters in cages.
   a. catch   b. kill   c. boil alive

_____ 7. Fishermen use **bait** to get lobsters to enter the cages.
   a. wooden poles   b. long ropes   c. food

_____ 8. A **float** shows the location of each cage.
   a. brightly colored object   b. object that does not sink   c. flag

A Second Look at Vocabulary

Complete the sentences. Use the words from the first exercise.

1. Just like a lobster, a turtle has a hard, strong _____.

2. The _____ of Maine is cold and wet during winter.

3. Fishermen use cages called "pots" to _____ lobsters.

4. Fishermen choose a _____ that lobsters like to eat.

5. A _____ stays on top of the ocean so fishermen know where to find their lobster cages.

6. A lobster uses its _____ to catch fish, snails, and other food.

7. Lobster, a _____ food, is costly to buy.

8. Fishermen, farmers, and other workers help build the _____ of Maine.

Understanding the Reading

Choose the best answer.

_____ 1. The fish and shellfish caught by Maine's fishermen are
    a. always served fresh.
    b. an important food for children, prisoners, and servants.
    c. a key to the economy of Maine.

_____ 2. The fishermen of Maine
    a. began catching lobsters about 20 years ago.
    b. catch more lobsters than fishermen of other states.
    c. must go far into the Atlantic to catch lobsters.

_____ 3. Lobsters use their claws to
    a. catch and eat food.
    b. swim rapidly after their food.
    c. walk on the bottom of the ocean.

_____ 4. Lobsters are usually boiled alive because
    a. they turn red when they are cooked.
    b. canned lobster is too expensive.
    c. lobster meat spoils quickly.

_____ 5. Fishermen catch lobsters
    a. with traps using dead fish as bait.
    b. with large nets.
    c. when they crawl onto land.

Why Did It Happen?

Match the sentence parts.

_____ 1. When a lobster loses some body parts,

_____ 2. When a lobster enters a "pot,"

_____ 3. Because Maine has 200 miles of coastline,

_____ 4. When a lobster is boiled,

_____ 5. Because millions of lobsters are caught in Maine,

a. it turns red.

b. fishing is important.

c. it cannot escape.

d. Maine's restaurants specialize in lobster.

e. it can grow them again.

What Do You Think?

Discuss these questions.

1. Why do you think that lobster became a luxury food?

2. Do you think lobster fishing in Maine is a good job? Why or why not?

3. Lobsters are boiled alive. Do you think that this is OK? Why or why not?

A Last Look

Write about one of these topics.

1. Why do many doctors tell people to eat more seafood and less red meat? Do research to learn more about the topic.

2. How much seafood do you eat? What kinds? Why do you or don't you eat it?

3. Some fishermen and scientists worry that there are not enough lobsters. Are too many being caught? Is throwing waste into the sea—pollution— killing lobsters? Do research to find out who's right.

Massachusetts

Thinking about the Picture

1. What clothes is this Pilgrim wearing?

2. Who were the Pilgrims? Where did they live? Where did they come from?

The Pilgrims

The first English settlers in Massachusetts were looking for religious freedom. They were "Separatists"—people who disagreed with the Church of England. To worship the way they wanted, they went first to Holland. Then they got permission to start their own colony in North America. Their leader, William Bradford, wrote that they "knew they were pilgrims." That is what most people now call them.

In September 1620, the Pilgrims sailed from Plymouth, England. Their little ship was the *Mayflower*. The trip across the Atlantic was long and difficult. Finally, after 66 days, they saw land. It was a long "arm" of land called Cape Cod. The Pilgrims landed and looked for a good place to settle. On December 21, 1620, they chose a place they called Plymouth. Before landing, the men signed an agreement, the *Mayflower* Compact. They agreed to make laws for the good of the colony.

The first winter was terrible. They had landed too late to plant crops. They had little food, except the animals they hunted. Half the colonists did not live through the first winter. They died of disease and cold.

In the spring, a Native American named Samoset arrived in Plymouth. Surprisingly, he spoke English. He had learned it from fishermen in Maine. Many of his people had also died from disease. Indians and settlers worked to help one another. Samoset introduced the Pilgrims to other Native Americans. One was Squanto, who had been a slave in Europe. Squanto helped the Pilgrims learn to hunt, grow corn, and catch seafood.

In October 1621, the Pilgrims shared a feast of thanksgiving with the local Indians. They probably ate wild fowl, fish, deer meat, oysters, and corn bread. The U.S. now celebrates Thanksgiving every November. The traditional meal includes turkey and pumpkin pie.

A First Look at Vocabulary

Match each term with its meaning.

_____	**1.** permission	a.	traveled by ship
_____	**2.** pilgrim	b.	gratefulness
_____	**3.** sailed	c.	one of the people who lived in America first
_____	**4.** colony	d.	serious illness
_____	**5.** landed	e.	agreement
_____	**6.** disease	f.	area under control of a distant country
_____	**7.** Native American	g.	person who travels for a religious reason
_____	**8.** feast	h.	in the way something was done in the past
_____	**9.** thanksgiving	i.	went on shore or land
_____	**10.** traditional	j.	large meal

A Second Look at Vocabulary

Complete the sentences. Use the words in the box.

colonies	feast	Native Americans	pilgrims	thanksgiving
disease	landed	permission	sailed	traditional

1. In the 1600s, people from England started _____ in America.

2. The king gave them _____ to make homes in America.

3. Reaching land after their long trip was a reason for _____.

4. The first people in Massachusetts were _____.

5. The travelers were _____ who wanted freedom of religion.

6. In the United States, turkey is a _____ food for Thanksgiving dinner.

7. They _____ across the ocean in a small ship.

8. Many different foods covered the table. It was a _____.

9. They _____ where flat, forested land came down to the sea.

10. A _____ made the Pilgrims sick.

Massachusetts

Understanding the Reading

Choose the best answer.

_____ **1.** The Pilgrims came to North America looking for
    a. religious freedom.
    b. farmland.
    c. Native Americans.

_____ **2.** The Pilgrims landed in America in
    a. 1492.
    b. 1620.
    c. 1861.

_____ **3.** Squanto showed the Pilgrims how to
    a. sail the _Mayflower_.
    b. hunt, grow corn, and catch seafood.
    c. protect themselves from the Native Americans.

Reading between the Lines

Look carefully at the reading. Mark each statement _T_ for _true_ or _F_ for _false_.

_____ **1.** The Separatists wanted to join the Church of England.

_____ **2.** The Pilgrims were not prepared for the first winter.

_____ **3.** Women were asked to sign the _Mayflower_ Compact.

_____ **4.** The Pilgrims were grateful to the Native Americans.

Why Did It Happen?

Match the sentence parts.

_____ **1.** The Separatists went to Holland

_____ **2.** In the _Mayflower_ Compact, the Pilgrims agreed

_____ **3.** The Pilgrims did not plant crops when they landed

_____ **4.** The Pilgrims held a feast

    a. because it was too late in the season.

    b. to celebrate their lives in the new land.

    c. to be free to worship.

    d. to make laws for the good of the colony.

What Do You Think?

Discuss these questions.

1. Would you have joined the Pilgrims when they came to America? Why or why not?

2. Why didn't the Pilgrims know how to hunt, grow corn, or catch seafood?

3. Do you celebrate Thanksgiving? What are your traditions for this holiday?

A Last Look

Write about one of these topics.

1. How could the Pilgrims have prepared better for their trip to America?

2. Squanto had been to Europe where he was a slave. Learn more about his life. Why did he want to help the Pilgrims?

Massachusetts

New Hampshire

Thinking about the Picture

1. How is Robert Frost dressed here? Do you expect poets to dress like this? Why or why not?
2. At what time in Frost's life was this picture taken?

Robert Frost

Robert Frost was one of America's favorite poets. Living on a farm in New Hampshire, he wrote about New England's people and land. Yet people everywhere can appreciate Frost's poetry. He used simple language to describe deep emotions. He explored connections between people and nature.

Robert Frost was born in San Francisco in 1874. When he was 11, his father died. His mother moved the family to Massachusetts, where her husband's family lived. Frost wrote his first poem when he was 16. While he was still in high school, Frost fell in love with Elinor White. He dropped out of Dartmouth College because school bored him. He just wanted to write poetry and be with Elinor. In 1894, he sold his first poem to a magazine for $15. He called it "My Butterfly: An Elegy." He and Elinor married in 1895. For a while, both taught in a school run by his mother.

In 1897 Frost went back to college at Harvard. He later dropped out because of illness. He turned to country life and moved to a farm in New Hampshire. When the farm failed, he went back to teaching and writing poetry. His poems did not sell, and in 1912 he took his family to England. British publishers liked his work and issued two books. British critics praised Frost's writing, and suddenly he was successful.

The Frost family returned to the United States in 1915 and bought a farm in New Hampshire. Frost's poetry became popular. Soon he was one of the best known writers in the United States.

In 1924, Frost won his first Pulitzer Prize for a book of poetry about New Hampshire. In the next decades, he won three more Pulitzer Prizes. In January 1961, he read his poem "The Gift Outright" at the inauguration of President John F. Kennedy. Frost died in 1963.

A First Look at Vocabulary

Choose the best definition for each word in bold type.

_____ 1. Many people **appreciate** Frost's poems.
      a. read   b. write about   c. think well of

_____ 2. **Emotions** are the subject of Frost's poems.
      a. beliefs   b. feelings   c. opinions

_____ 3. Robert Frost saw **connections** between people and nature.
      a. relationships   b. conflicts   c. deep love

_____ 4. Robert Frost **dropped out** of college.
      a. continued in   b. stopped attending   c. enjoyed

_____ 5. Frost became **bored** at college.
      a. unsuccessful   b. unpopular   c. not interested

_____ 6. The **publishers** liked Frost's poems.
      a. salespeople   b. teachers at colleges   c. companies that make books

_____ 7. People **praised** Frost for his thoughtful poems.
      a. disliked   b. wrote about   c. said good things about

_____ 8. The **inauguration** of President John Kennedy was in January 1961.
      a. election   b. murder   c. ceremony starting a term of office

A Second Look at Vocabulary

Complete the sentences. Use the words from the first exercise.

1. Did Robert Frost _____ living close to nature in the country?

2. Some people see _____ between Henry Wadsworth Longfellow and Robert Frost.

3. John Kennedy asked Frost to read a poem at his _____ .

4. The young woman _____ of college to take care of her sick mother.

5. The mayor _____ the firefighters because they saved three children.

6. This movie was so interesting! I was never _____ by it.

7. Frost felt strongly about nature and shared those _____ in his poems.

8. Frost sold his first two books to _____ when he lived in England.

Understanding the Reading

Choose the best answer.

_____ **1.** When Frost's father died, his family moved to
   a. New Hampshire.
   b. Massachusetts.
   c. England.

_____ **2.** Frost first dropped out of school because he was bored. Later he dropped out because he
   a. wanted to get married.
   b. wanted to write poetry.
   c. became sick.

_____ **3.** As a young man, Frost earned his living as a farmer and
   a. teacher.
   b. publisher.
   c. critic.

_____ **4.** Frost first became popular in
   a. New Hampshire.
   b. Massachusetts.
   c. England.

Fact or Opinion?

Mark each statement _F_ for _fact_ or _O_ for _opinion_.

_____ **1.** Frost was wrong to drop out of college.

_____ **2.** British critics thought Frost was a fine poet.

_____ **3.** Country life is an important subject in Frost's poetry.

When Did It Happen?

Write numbers to put the events in the order they happened.

_____ Robert Frost won his first Pulitzer Prize.

_____ Frost read his poem "The Gift Outright" at President Kennedy's inauguration.

_____ Robert Frost married Elinor.

_____ Frost moved to England.

What Do You Think?
Discuss these questions.

1. Do you like to read poetry? Why or why not?

2. Frost wrote about the lives of ordinary people in the U.S. Why would his poetry interest people in England?

3. Who is your favorite poet? Why?

A Last Look
Write about one of these topics.

1. Read Frost's poem, "The Gift Outright." Was this a good poem to read at a president's inauguration? Why or why not?

2. Why was Robert Frost so popular with people in the United States?

3. Write a poem about the area where you live. Choose an everyday subject and use ordinary people.

Rhode Island

Thinking about the Picture
1. Who is shown in this picture? What might they be discussing?
2. Why would Roger Williams found a settlement?

The Fight for Religious Freedom

 The first settlers in New England wanted to worship in their own way. They could not do that in England. But the Puritans in Massachusetts welcomed only their own beliefs. That led to the founding of a new colony. It grew into the state of Rhode Island.

Roger Williams was educated in England as a minister. Soon he began to disagree with the teachings of the Church of England. He moved to Massachusetts in 1631 but soon argued with the Puritan leaders there, too. He said that government and religion should be separate. Puritan leaders ordered Williams to stop spreading his ideas. When he refused, they forced him to leave. In 1636, Williams and some friends bought land from Native Americans. They founded a settlement named Providence. In 1643, the English king gave Williams permission to found a colony.

The news spread that the new colony was safe for people with different beliefs. Other people from Massachusetts moved there and started new towns. In 1657, Quakers came from other colonies. Spanish and Portuguese Jews arrived in 1658. They later built the first synagogue in North America at Newport. French Protestants settled in Rhode Island in 1686. Roman Catholic rulers made life in France dangerous for them.

Rhode Island also led in other steps to freedom. In the early 1700s, slavery was legal in all the colonies. New England had fewer slaves than other regions because most people had only small farms. But Quakers in Rhode Island wanted to end slavery completely. In 1774, it was the first colony to ban the importing of slaves. In 1784, a law said that the children of slaves would become free. By 1807, there were no more slaves in the state.

Rhode Island was the last colony to approve the new U.S. Constitution. Its delegates waited until 1790, when the Bill of Rights was ready to be added. It guaranteed basic rights such as freedom of speech and religion.

A First Look at Vocabulary

Choose the best definition for each word in bold type.

_____ **1.** Many Christians go to church to **worship.**
    a. give thanks   b. pray   c. show respect for God

_____ **2.** Roger Williams was trained as a **minister.**
    a. religious leader   b. government leader   c. military leader

_____ **3.** Williams was not the only person to **disagree** with the Puritans.
    a. compare people   b. have different opinions   c. think the same

_____ **4.** The Puritans did not want Williams **spreading** his ideas of religious freedom.
    a. sharing   b. believing   c. practicing

_____ **5.** Roger Williams **refused** to stop saying that government and church should be separate.
    a. said "no"   b. asked   c. agreed

_____ **6.** The city of Providence was **founded** by Roger Williams.
    a. named   b. started   c. discovered

_____ **7.** The Jewish people built a **synagogue** in Newport.
    a. government building   b. school   c. building for worship

_____ **8.** Many people wanted **slavery** to end.
    a. owning another person   b. being in prison   c. serving in the army

A Second Look at Vocabulary

Complete the sentences. Use the words from the first exercise.

1. News of Williams's new colony began _____ through America.

2. Was Williams the only one to _____ with the Puritans?

3. The first _____ in America was built by Jewish people of Rhode Island.

4. People of Rhode Island disliked _____. They did not believe one person should own another.

5. Some people _____ to join Williams.

6. People from Europe _____ many colonies in America.

7. In the U.S., religious people are free to _____ in any way they want.

8. Williams was educated as a _____ in the Church of England.

Understanding the Reading

Choose the best answer.

_____ 1. The Puritans wanted to worship in their own way, but they
     a. welcomed people of all religions.
     b. gave other people freedom of religion, too.
     c. did not give freedom of religion to others.

_____ 2. Roger Williams left England and Massachusetts because
     a. he disagreed with the religious teachings.
     b. they permitted slavery.
     c. he wanted to found his own colony.

_____ 3. Quakers, Jews, and French Protestants settled in Rhode Island because
     a. land was cheap.
     b. they could follow their own religious beliefs.
     c. they could build their businesses.

_____ 4. In the 1700s, many people in Rhode Island were free, but not
     a. slaves.
     b. Quakers.
     c. Jews.

_____ 5. Roger Williams and his friends founded the city of Providence. They bought the land from
     a. the Puritans.
     b. the king of England.
     c. Native Americans.

When Did It Happen?

Write numbers to put the events in the order they happened.

_____ French Protestants settled in Rhode Island.

_____ Rhode Island made a law against importing slaves.

_____ Roger Williams founded Providence.

_____ Puritans settled in New England.

_____ Puritans forced Roger Williams to leave Massachusetts.

_____ Slavery ended in Rhode Island.

What Do You Think?
Discuss these questions.

1. Why do you suppose the Puritans did not allow freedom of religion in Massachusetts?

2. In 1784, the people of Rhode Island said that the children of slaves would become free. If people disagreed with slavery, why didn't they free all slaves?

A Last Look
Write about one of these topics.

1. What are some countries today that do not allow religious freedom? Why don't they allow people to worship as they wish?

2. Do research to learn about the Quakers. Why were they against slavery? What did they do to end slavery?

Vermont

Thinking about the Picture

1. Ethan Allen holds a sword. What does that tell you about him?
2. Look at Allen's face, how he stands, and how he holds his arms. What kind of person do you think he was?

The Green Mountain Boys

The name *Vermont* comes from the French words for "green mountain." It refers to the thick evergreen forests on the hills. In the 1700s, a colorful group of settlers fought to keep the Vermont region independent. They were called the Green Mountain Boys.

The quarrel began before the American Revolution. No one was sure of the exact boundaries of this frontier area. The colonies of New York and New Hampshire both claimed it. Between 1749 and 1763, the colonial governor of New Hampshire gave out 131 grants of land west of the Connecticut River. They were called the "New Hampshire Grants."

But in 1764, the British government gave the region to New York. It ordered settlers in the New Hampshire Grants to give up their land or pay New York for it. New York then gave out land grants for the same region. The first settlers fought to keep their land. Ethan Allen and his brothers organized an armed militia, known as the Green Mountain Boys. They attacked New York settlers and burned their cabins. In April 1775, they sent a petition to the King of England. They asked for their own government.

A week later, settlers in Massachusetts had a battle with British troops. It was the start of the American Revolution. For the people of Vermont, the British—not New Yorkers—were now the enemy. In May 1775, Ethan Allen and the Green Mountain Boys made a surprise attack on Fort Ticonderoga. They captured the British fort and its cannon. In August 1777, the militia group won again at the battle of Bennington.

Also in 1777, the settlers in the Green Mountains set up an independent republic. They decided to call it "Vermont." In 1790, Vermont finally ended the quarrel with New York. It paid the state $30,000 for the land. Vermont became the 14th state in 1791.

A First Look at Vocabulary

Match each term with its meaning.

_____ 1. quarrel   a. army

_____ 2. frontier   b. said they owned

_____ 3. claimed   c. disagreement; fight

_____ 4. militia   d. a strongly built place defended by soldiers

_____ 5. petition   e. a written paper asking for something

_____ 6. captured   f. took by force

_____ 7. fort   g. a country where people choose representatives

_____ 8. republic   h. border between a settled and a wild area

A Second Look at Vocabulary

Choose the best answer to complete each sentence.

_____ 1. Before Vermont was a state, it was an independent _____.
     a. colony   b. county   c. republic

_____ 2. Wild animals and thick forests bordered the towns on the _____.
     a. frontier   b. grants   c. republic

_____ 3. Ethan Allen _____ land in the Green Mountains for his farm.
     a. attacked   b. refused   c. claimed

_____ 4. The troops built a strong _____ with high walls.
     a. cannon   b. territory   c. fort

_____ 5. The _____ asked the king for land.
     a. grant   b. petition   c. frontier

_____ 6. The army fought a hard battle and _____ the town.
     a. organized   b. quarreled   c. captured

_____ 7. The Vermont and New York settlers _____ over the land grants.
     a. quarreled   b. captured   c. organized

_____ 8. Men joined the _____ to fight in the American Revolution.
     a. militia   b. fort   c. republic

Understanding the Reading

Choose the best answer.

_____ 1. In French, the name *Vermont* means
   a. "tall forests."
   b. "green mountain."
   c. "many lakes."

_____ 2. The Green Mountain Boys wanted to
   a. make Vermont part of New York.
   b. make Vermont part of New Hampshire.
   c. make Vermont independent.

_____ 3. The British government decided that the people of Vermont had to leave their land or buy it from
   a. New York.
   b. New Hampshire.
   c. the king of England.

_____ 4. The Green Mountain Boys captured a British fort called
   a. Ticonderoga.
   b. Lake Champlain.
   c. Connecticut.

_____ 5. Vermont became the
   a. first colony.
   b. 13th state.
   c. 14th state.

Reading between the Lines

Look carefully at the reading. Mark each statement *T* for *true* or *F* for *false*.

_____ 1. The Green Mountain Boys were unimportant in early American history.

_____ 2. Vermont became a state only after fighting for its land.

_____ 3. The petition to the king of England was too late.

_____ 4. New York lost the quarrel with Vermont.

_____ 5. The quarrel between New York, New Hampshire, and Vermont was all about land.

What Do You Think?
Discuss these questions.

1. Why do you suppose the settlers from two colonies fought for the Green Mountains?

2. Vermont was an independent republic. Why do you think it gave up its independence to join the United States?

A Last Look
Write about one of these topics.

1. Look up Fort Ticonderoga. Why was the capture of this fort important?

2. Learn about the life of Ethan Allen. What happened to him after the American Revolution?

3. Look up the Green Mountains. What kind of area is it today? Are the mountains still forested? What do people there do?

Mid-Atlantic Region

Delaware, District of Columbia, Maryland, New Jersey, Virginia, West Virginia

A Quick Look at this Region

In the early 1600s, the Dutch, Swedes, and English all set up colonies in the Mid-Atlantic region. The area had fertile land, thick forests, and wide, deep rivers. Its climate was moderate. Later, England took over the colonies. The first Africans were brought to the colonies in the 1600s. They were servants and slaves.

The region developed as a center for agriculture and industry. In the 1800s, more immigrants arrived. Most came from southern and eastern Europe. In the late 20th century, immigrants from Asia and Puerto Rico added to the region's diversity.

The District of Columbia shared in the history of this region, but it is not part of any state. It was built as the center for the government of the United States. It is on land between Maryland and Virginia.

Today the Mid-Atlantic region is a center for government, education, and industry. Farming is important in some areas. Tourists come to the region to visit sites where history was made, like the White House, Harpers Ferry, and Thomas Edison's laboratory.

Delaware

Thinking about the Picture

1. Settlers from Sweden built houses like this one. Why do you think that they chose this kind of house?
2. What was life like in a house like this?

The Log Cabin

The first permanent settlers in what is now Delaware came from Sweden. In 1638 they set up a colony called "New Sweden." It included part of present-day New Jersey. This was Sweden's only American colony, but they were the first in North America to build log cabins. Like Sweden, North America had large forests. So the Swedish settlers built cabins like those they knew in their homeland.

When trees are chopped down, their round trunks can be cut quickly into logs. The Swedish settlers piled logs on top of each other to make the walls of the cabins. They cut the ends of the logs to fit tightly together at the corners. They filled spaces between the logs with stones or pieces of wood. Then they covered over cracks with mud, so the wind could not come in. Log cabins were warmer than the houses that settlers built in other colonies.

Later, immigrants from other countries moved into the Delaware River Valley. From the Swedish colonists, they learned how to build log cabins. People in other places also copied the practical Swedish homes. As pioneers moved westward, the log cabin became a popular type of house.

The settlers in New Sweden laid the foundation for the modern state of Delaware. They built a fort near the Delaware River. It was called Fort Christina, after the Swedish queen. The city of Wilmington, Delaware, grew up at the site of Fort Christina.

The Swedish colony lasted only a few years. Its main rival was the Dutch settlement at nearby New Amsterdam (now New York). In 1651, the Dutch built Fort Casimir (where New Castle, Delaware, is now). The Swedes captured that fort three years later, but the Dutch took it back in 1655. The Dutch also captured Fort Christina. The Swedish colonists continued their way of life, but the days of New Sweden were over. It soon became part of the English colony of Delaware.

A First Look at Vocabulary

Choose the best definition for each word in bold type.

_____ 1. The settlers **chopped** down trees to build log cabins.
     a. burned   b. found   c. cut

_____ 2. Logs for the cabin came from the **trunks** of large trees.
     a. leaves and branches   b. main part of trees   c. wood

_____ 3. Other pioneers **copied** the Swedish homes.
     a. made the same kind   b. studied   c. changed

_____ 4. Log cabins were **practical** on the frontier.
     a. useful   b. new   c. costly

_____ 5. The Swedish **pioneers** lived in log cabins.
     a. explorers   b. early settlers   c. leaders

_____ 6. The **foundation** for the United States was made by the early settlers.
     a. government   b. supporting base   c. settlements

_____ 7. The city of Wilmington now stands on the **site** of Fort Christina.
     a. exact place   b. history   c. flat place

_____ 8. Europeans started many **settlements** in North America.
     a. villages   b. military bases   c. businesses

A Second Look at Vocabulary

Complete the sentences. Use the words from the first exercise.

1. The _____ built new homes on the frontier.

2. Today, New York City is at the _____ of New Amsterdam.

3. Many settlers found out that log cabins were _____.

4. Because the trees were old, their _____ were very thick.

5. Over the years, the pioneers built many _____.

6. The settlers _____ down trees to make space for farms.

7. People have _____ the Swedish log cabins for hundreds of years.

8. Farmers were the _____ of the early settlements.

Understanding the Reading

Choose the best answer.

_____ **1.** The first European settlement in Delaware was called
    a. New Amsterdam.
    b. Fort Casimir.
    c. New Sweden.

_____ **2.** The Swedish settlers were the first pioneers to build
    a. forts.
    b. log cabins.
    c. settlements.

_____ **3.** Fort Christina was captured by
    a. the Swedes.
    b. the Dutch.
    c. Native Americans.

Why Did It Happen?

Match the sentence parts.

_____ **1.** Swedes built log cabins at home,

_____ **2.** Delaware had large forests,

_____ **3.** Log cabins were practical,

_____ **4.** Swedish settlers filled spaces between logs,

a. so other settlers copied the idea.

b. so they built them in New Sweden.

c. so that the wind could not come in.

d. so settlers had logs to use for cabins.

When Did It Happen?

Write numbers to put the events in the order they happened.

_____ The colony of New Sweden came to an end.

_____ The Swedes captured Fort Casimir.

_____ The Swedes built Fort Christina.

_____ The Dutch captured Fort Christina.

What Do You Think?

Discuss these questions.

1. Why did Sweden and other European countries want colonies in North America?

2. New Sweden was captured by the Dutch. How do you think the settlers of New Sweden felt?

3. Do you think it would be easy to build a log cabin? Why or why not?

A Last Look

Write about one of these topics.

1. Learn about the climate in Sweden and the climate in Delaware. How are the two alike and different?

2. Sometimes people still build log cabins. Find out about modern log cabins. Would you like to live in one?

District of Columbia

Thinking about the Picture

1. Do you expect the president of a country to live in a house like this? Why or why not?

2. Would you like to visit the White House? Why?

The White House

The United States government first moved to Washington, D.C., in 1800. Many buildings in the new capital were not finished.

Before 1800, the federal government met in New York City. The first president, George Washington, took his oath of office there. John Adams became the nation's second president in 1797. In Washington, D.C., workmen were still finishing "the President's House." Adams and his family were the first to live there. The building was built of gray-white limestone, but it was not yet called the White House.

In 1812, war broke out between the United States and Great Britain. In August 1814, President James Madison left the city to meet his troops. The British came nearer. Madison's wife, Dolley, knew she had to flee the President's House. She rescued government papers and a famous picture of George Washington. The British army marched into Washington and set the city on fire. Both the Capitol and the President's House were burned.

After the war, the President's House was rebuilt. The stone was painted white. That was a contrast with the many red brick buildings in Washington. Many people began to call it "the white house." It was also known as "the Executive Mansion." In 1901, when Theodore Roosevelt was president, the words *White House* appeared on official stationery for the first time.

The White House has 132 rooms and 35 bathrooms. Several beautiful rooms are used for ceremonies and official events. The State Dining Room can seat as many as 140 guests. The president and most official staff occupy the West Wing. The president works in the Oval Office. The First Lady has an office in the East Wing. The family's private quarters are on the second floor. Some public rooms are open for special tours by military and school groups. The White House web site offers an online tour of the Blue Room, the Green Room, and others.

A First Look at Vocabulary

Match each term with its meaning.

_____ 1. capital   a. a comparison showing differences

_____ 2. federal government   b. walked together as soldiers do

_____ 3. oath of office   c. writing paper

_____ 4. broke out   d. city where the government is

_____ 5. flee   e. central government

_____ 6. marched   f. the building in which the U.S. Congress meets

_____ 7. Capitol   g. promise someone makes when starting a government job

_____ 8. contrast   h. formal acts on special occasions

_____ 9. stationery   i. run away from

_____ 10. ceremonies   j. started

A Second Look at Vocabulary

Complete the sentences. Use the words from the first exercise.

1. The president wrote a letter on his official _____.

2. The president of the United States takes the _____ on January 20.

3. Washington, D.C., is the _____ of the United States.

4. Congress meets in the _____, not in the White House.

5. The _____ has more power than any one state government.

6. World War II _____ in 1939, but the United States entered the war in 1941.

7. As the enemy army came closer, people started to _____ the city.

8. The army _____ along the street to the beat of drums.

9. In _____ to Delaware, the District of Columbia is not a state.

10. The president welcomed the foreign leaders in _____ at the White House.

District of Columbia

Understanding the Reading

Choose the best answer.

_____ **1.** The first president to live in the White House was
   a. Theodore Roosevelt.
   b. George Washington.
   c. John Adams.

_____ **2.** The British burned the President's House because
   a. they were fighting a war with the United States.
   b. they wanted to kill the president.
   c. it was moved from New York to Washington, D.C.

_____ **3.** People in the U.S. can
   a. visit the White House whenever they want to.
   b. sometimes visit the White House with special groups.
   c. never visit the White House.

When Did It Happen?

Write numbers to put the events in the order they happened.

_____ The federal government moved to Washington, D.C.

_____ George Washington took his oath of office as president.

_____ People began to call the President's House "the white house."

_____ The British burned the President's House.

Reading between the Lines

Look carefully at the reading. Mark each statement _T_ for _true_ or _F_ for _false_.

_____ **1.** The President's House was built of gray-white limestone.

_____ **2.** John Adams was president when the British set fire to Washington, D.C.

_____ **3.** Theodore Roosevelt thought "White House" was a good name for the president's home.

_____ **4.** The government does not give the public much information about the White House.

What Do You Think?
Discuss these questions.

1. Most people never go inside the White House. But they can see some rooms on the White House web site. Have you ever taken a "virtual tour" online? Describe it.

2. Do you think ordinary people should be able to visit the White House? Give reasons for your answer.

3. The White House is a luxurious building. Should the president of the United States live in such an expensive house?

A Last Look
Write about one of these topics.

1. The federal government decided not to put the capital in one of the states. Instead, the government made the District of Columbia and built a new city. Do research to learn why the government did this. Was it a good idea?

2. Find Washington, D.C., on a map. Is this a good place for the U.S. capital? Why do you think this place was chosen? What place would you choose? Why?

District of Columbia

Maryland

Thinking about the Picture

1. What symbols are on the U.S. flag? What do they mean?
2. What is the purpose of a national flag?

The Star-Spangled Banner

 The national anthem of the United States is "The Star-Spangled Banner." The title refers to the U.S. flag. Its square blue "field" is scattered, or "spangled," with stars, which represent the states. A Maryland lawyer named Francis Scott Key wrote the words of this song. He was inspired by a flag that flew over Fort McHenry, near Baltimore, Maryland.

Francis Scott Key was born in Maryland in 1779 and grew up on his family's estate. He went to school in Maryland, then became a lawyer in the nearby District of Columbia. Key was also a musician and poet.

In 1812, Great Britain and the United States went to war. In 1814, the British captured Washington, D.C., and burned the Capitol and the White House. In the attack, they captured Dr. William Beanes, a friend of Key's. They kept him prisoner on a warship in Chesapeake Bay. On September 13, 1814, Key and a government official sailed to the ship to bargain for Beanes's release. The British agreed to let him go. But they had already planned to attack Fort McHenry, which protected Baltimore. Key and his friends had to stay on the ship until the attack was over.

The fierce British attack went on all night. Key watched from the ship. He saw "bombs bursting in air" and "rockets' red glare" in the night sky. At dawn on September 14, Key could finally see the huge flag flying over the fort. It was the U.S. flag, with 15 stars and 15 stripes. The U.S. still held the fort!

The bravery of the fort's defenders inspired him to write his famous poem. It was first printed under the title "The Defense of Fort McHenry." Soon newspapers all over the United States were printing the poem. Key's words were set to the tune of a popular drinking song. Soon the song gained a new title, "The Star-Spangled Banner." The Union Army sang it during the Civil War. It was the military's official song in World War I. Finally, Congress made it the national anthem on March 3, 1931.

A First Look at Vocabulary

Choose the best definition for each word in bold type.

_____ 1. The **national anthem** was written after a battle.
      a. fighting song   b. school song   c. song of a country

_____ 2. The battle **inspired** Francis Scott Key.
      a. caused a strong feeling b. made happy   c. frightened

_____ 3. Key grew up on his family's **estate** in Maryland.
      a. business   b. land with a house   c. city apartment

_____ 4. Key's friend was a **prisoner** of the British.
      a. soldier   b. enemy   c. captured person

_____ 5. Key tried to **bargain** with the British captain.
      a. make an agreement   b. get away from   c. fight against

_____ 6. Key wanted his friend's **release.**
      a. estate   b. freedom   c. help

_____ 7. The battle was **fiercely** fought.
      a. quickly   b. hardly   c. violently

_____ 8. The flag inspired Key with **patriotism.**
      a. love of country   b. fear of war   c. joy in living

A Second Look at Vocabulary

Complete the sentences. Use the words from the first exercise.

1. After the war was over, the prisoners finally got their _____.

2. The _____ is sung at many sporting events.

3. The _____ had a large house, many fields, and pastures.

4. The defenders fought _____ and finally won the battle.

5. The _____ was locked in a small room.

6. Because of _____, some people want to help others in their country.

7. The great speech _____ everyone who heard it.

8. At garage sales, people often _____ for a lower price.

Understanding the Reading

Choose the best answer.

_____ **1.** What was Francis Scott Key's profession?
  a. He was a soldier.
  b. He was a farmer.
  c. He was a lawyer.

_____ **2.** Why did Key go onto a British warship?
  a. He wanted to free his friend, William Beanes.
  b. He wanted to stop the British attack.
  c. He wanted to return home to Great Britain.

_____ **3.** What did Key see during the night?
  a. He saw British bombs and rockets exploding.
  b. He saw nothing because of the darkness and rain.
  c. He saw the U.S. flag flying over the fort.

_____ **4.** What did Key see on the morning after the battle?
  a. He saw the British flag flying over the fort.
  b. He saw the U.S. flag still flying.
  c. He saw the fort on fire.

_____ **5.** Where did the music for the U.S. national anthem come from?
  a. Key wrote the music.
  b. It came from a drinking song.
  c. Key's friend, William Beanes, wrote the music.

Why Did It Happen?

Match the sentence parts.

_____ **1.** Key had to stay on the warship,

   a. so people began to sing it.

_____ **2.** Key saw the U.S. flag flying at dawn,

   b. so he knew the U.S. forces still had the fort.

_____ **3.** Key was inspired by the brave defense,

   c. so Congress made it the national anthem.

_____ **4.** Key's poem was set to music,

   d. so he watched the British attack Fort McHenry.

_____ **5.** The song was popular for many years,

   e. so he wrote a poem about the battle.

What Do You Think?

Discuss these questions.

1. Was it dangerous for Francis Scott Key to go to the British warship? Why do you think he went there? Was he brave or foolish?

2. What kind of events inspire you? Have you ever written something because you felt inspired? What happened?

A Last Look

Write about one of these topics.

1. What is the national anthem of your native country? What do the words say? Is it a good anthem for the country? Why or why not?

2. If you wrote a national anthem for the United States, what would you write about? Why?

Maryland

33

New Jersey

Thinking about the Picture

1. What do you know about Edison from his clothing?
2. Does this man look like one of the world's greatest inventors? Why or why not?

Thomas Alva Edison

People often called Thomas Alva Edison "the wizard of Menlo Park." This town in New Jersey was home to Edison's laboratory and workshop. He made some of his most important inventions there. They changed life around the world.

Edison was born on February 11, 1847, in Milan, Ohio. When he was 7, his family moved to Port Huron, Michigan. He went to school for only a short time. After that, his mother taught him at home. Edison was curious and ambitious. He spent his spare time in the library, reading. At age 16, Edison took a job sending telegraph messages. He was bored, so he found a way to send messages automatically while he was asleep. That was his first practical invention.

In 1868, Edison moved east to try to sell his inventions. On Wall Street, New York's financial district, he fixed a machine that kept track of gold prices. He repaired and made other business machines. Those skills and ideas brought him $40,000. Edison used the money to open a workshop in Newark, New Jersey. In 1876, he moved the workshop to Menlo Park.

Edison made important improvements in the telephone and typewriter, which others had invented. In 1877, he invented the phonograph. That made him famous. In 1879 came the first practical incandescent lightbulb. Edison also set up a power station that supplied electricity in New York City. He worked on cameras and projectors, which helped start the motion-picture industry. He also invented or improved the cement mixer, a vote-counting machine, an early copy machine, and a dictating machine. Edison held U.S. patents for almost 1,100 inventions. (A patent is a government document. It gives an inventor the right to make and sell a product.)

Edison received many awards, from both the United States government and other countries. He died in 1931 in West Orange, New Jersey.

A First Look at Vocabulary

Match each term with its meaning.

_____ **1.** wizard   a. new things

_____ **2.** laboratory   b. having a strong desire to succeed

_____ **3.** inventions   c. glass object that gives off light

_____ **4.** ambitious   d. without human help

_____ **5.** telegraph   e. official paper

_____ **6.** automatically   f. permission to make and sell a product

_____ **7.** improvements   g. magician

_____ **8.** lightbulb   h. changes that make something better

_____ **9.** patent   i. machine that sends messages by electric signal

_____ **10.** document   j. place where a scientist works

A Second Look at Vocabulary

Complete the sentences. Use the words from the first exercise.

1. Thomas Edison was called a _____ because he invented so many amazing things.

2. In the U.S. today, most people use the telephone, the fax machine, and e-mail instead of the _____.

3. A _____ helps an inventor make money from an invention.

4. The _____ makes it easier to read after sunset.

5. Cashiers use bar-code scanners to read prices _____.

6. My home is pretty good, but I'd like to make some _____.

7. Two of Edison's most important _____ were the phonograph and the lightbulb.

8. The inventor's _____ was full of half-finished inventions.

9. An _____ person works hard to succeed.

10. A marriage license is one kind of _____.

Understanding the Reading

Choose the best answer.

_____ **1.** Thomas Edison
    a. spent very little time in school.
    b. studied many years in school and college.
    c. only finished high school.

_____ **2.** Edison went to New York to
    a. sell his inventions.
    b. begin his work as an inventor.
    c. get a patent on his inventions.

_____ **3.** Edison's Menlo Park laboratory was in
    a. Ohio.
    b. Michigan.
    c. New Jersey.

_____ **4.** Edison's first practical invention could
    a. record people speaking.
    b. send telegraph messages automatically.
    c. count votes.

_____ **5.** Edison invented or improved
    a. the microwave, ultrasound, and X-ray.
    b. the Internet, cell phone, and compact disk.
    c. the typewriter, telephone, and phonograph.

Where's the Idea?

These are main ideas from the reading. Write the number of the paragraph where you find each idea.

_____ Edison had little schooling, but he was curious and ambitious.

_____ Edison made many inventions and changed the world.

_____ Edison received many awards.

_____ Edison invented many machines and improved many others.

_____ Edison moved east, made money, and started a workshop.

What Do You Think?

Discuss these questions.

1. Can someone with little schooling succeed as an inventor today? Why or why not?

2. What are Edison's three most important inventions or improvements? Explain your choices.

A Last Look

Write about one of these topics.

1. What is an important invention that you would like to see? Describe the invention and tell how it would help people.

2. Tell about another inventor you know about. What did he or she invent?

Virginia

Thinking about the Picture

1. Why is George Washington remembered today?
2. What do you know about Washington's life?
3. What are some places that are named for him?

Father of His Country

 Virginia was the home of many early U.S. leaders. George Washington may be the most famous. He led the colonial army to victory in the American Revolution. He was the new nation's first president. People saw him as a wise statesman, "father of his country."

Washington was born in Westmoreland, Virginia, on February 22, 1732. He was educated mainly at home, then worked as a surveyor. When he was 20, he became an officer in the militia. At the time, Britain and France were fighting for lands in America. The French and Indian Wars lasted from 1754 to 1763. Washington showed that he could command soldiers.

Washington inherited the family plantation, Mount Vernon. He went back to Virginia. In 1759 he married Martha Dandridge Custis. She was a rich widow with two children. For some years, Washington lived the life of a wealthy farmer. He also served in the Virginia legislature.

By the early 1770s, American colonists were beginning to resent British rule. Some leaders decided it was time to fight for independence. They chose Washington as commander of the colonial army. He led the army from 1775 until the war ended. Most soldiers were untrained. Uniforms, gunpowder, and food were scarce. Many believed that only Washington could keep the army together.

The bitter cold winter of 1777–1778 was the lowest point. Washington's soldiers slept in icy tents at Valley Forge, Pennsylvania. More than 2,500 died of disease, hunger, and cold. Then help came from the French government. With that help, Washington's army won victory in 1781.

After the war ended, Washington went home to Mount Vernon. In 1787, he signed the Constitution of the new United States. He was then elected the nation's first president. After two terms, he returned happily to Mount Vernon. He died there on December 14, 1799.

A First Look at Vocabulary

Match each term with its meaning.

_____ **1.** surveyor   a. wife of a man who died

_____ **2.** inherited   b. temporary cloth shelters

_____ **3.** widow   c. soldier who is in charge

_____ **4.** legislature   d. not taught a job

_____ **5.** resent   e. someone who measures land

_____ **6.** commander   f. feel angry about

_____ **7.** untrained   g. chosen by voting

_____ **8.** gunpowder   h. got from a relative who died

_____ **9.** tents   i. material that explodes to shoot bullets

_____ **10.** elected   j. branch of government that makes laws

A Second Look at Vocabulary

Complete the sentences. Use the words from the box.

commander	gunpowder	legislature	surveyor	untrained
elect	inherited	resented	tents	widow

1. Without _____ for their guns, the soldiers could not fight well.

2. The new workers were _____, but they soon learned their jobs.

3. Many rich people _____ their money from their families.

4. The colonial government chose Washington as _____ of the army.

5. In the U.S., citizens _____ the government.

6. The man who died left behind a _____ and three children.

7. A _____ can tell where one farm ends and the next begins.

8. Congress is the _____ of the United States.

9. The colonists _____ British rule.

10. _____ were the only shelter the refugees had.

Understanding the Reading

Choose the best answer.

_____ 1. During the French and Indian Wars, Washington
   a. was elected president.
   b. showed that he could command soldiers.
   c. worked as a surveyor.

_____ 2. George Washington's plantation was called
   a. Mount Vernon.
   b. Valley Forge.
   c. Westmoreland.

_____ 3. George Washington was commander of the colonial army during the
   a. Civil War.
   b. American Revolution.
   c. French and Indian Wars.

_____ 4. The army Washington commanded
   a. was not able to defeat the British.
   b. was never defeated in battle.
   c. was untrained and had little food and gunpowder.

_____ 5. George Washington was
   a. the first president of the United States.
   b. chosen president by the legislature.
   c. elected king before he became president.

When Did It Happen?

Write numbers to put the events in the order they happened.

_____ Washington kept his army together during the winter of 1777–1778 at Valley Forge.

_____ Washington led soldiers in the French and Indian Wars.

_____ The French helped in the American Revolution.

_____ Washington was made commander of the army.

_____ Washington's army defeated the British in 1781.

What Do You Think?
Discuss these questions.

1. Was General Washington's job more difficult than the jobs of U.S. generals after him? Why do you think so?

2. Do you think Washington should be called "father of his country"? Why or why not?

A Last Look
Write about one of these topics.

1. Learn about Mount Vernon today. Does it still look as it did when Washington lived there? What do people see when they visit it?

2. Would you want one of your children to grow up to be president of the United States? Why or why not?

West Virginia

Thinking about the Picture

1. This building was used as a fort in 1859. Would this be a safe place to fight off enemies? Why do you think so?

2. Why is it important to save places like this?

Separation from Virginia

In the 1700s, life was very different in eastern and western Virginia. In the east, there were old towns and large plantations. Many wealthy landowners owned slaves. In the west was the rugged frontier. Settlers fought with Native Americans for the land.

In 1776, the American colonies became independent states. Virginia wrote a state constitution. It gave voting rights to white men who owned 25 acres of land. The men in the western region were angry. Most were small landowners or owned no land at all. That meant they could not vote. As early as 1829, they talked about separating from the east.

In 1850, all white men in Virginia got the right to vote, but there was another issue. People in the two regions also disagreed over slavery. Many settlers in the western part of Virginia were abolitionists. They wanted to end slavery in the U.S. In eastern Virginia, slavery was a way of life.

The most famous and violent abolitionist in Virginia was John Brown. In 1859, he led an attack on a government arsenal in the town of Harpers Ferry. Brown hoped to start a slave rebellion. He and his men captured the arsenal and took hostages. Later, Brown was tried for murder and treason and was hanged.

In 1860, Abraham Lincoln was elected president. Soon after, some southern states seceded from the Union. They formed the Confederate States of America. In April 1861, fighting broke out between Confederate and Union troops. Most of the southern states then left the Union. Virginia voted to join them in the Confederacy.

The delegates from western Virginia disagreed. In August 1861, they voted to stay in the Union. The western part would separate from Virginia and create a new state. Congress agreed to admit it. On June 20, 1863, West Virginia became the 35th state.

West Virginia

A First Look at Vocabulary

Choose the word that matches each definition in bold type.

_____ **1.** A farm with only 25 **measures of land** is not a large one.
    a. regions   b. mountains   c. acres

_____ **2.** Slavery was an **important matter** for the people of Virginia.
    a. rebellion   b. issue   c. arsenal

_____ **3.** **People who were against slavery** disagree with owners of slaves.
    a. writers   b. abolitionists   c. landowners

_____ **4.** U.S. soldiers guarded the **storehouse for weapons.**
    a. Confederacy   b. plantation   c. arsenal

_____ **5.** Many people feared a **war against the government.**
    a. treason   b. rebellion   c. attack

_____ **6.** John Brown was tried for **hurting his country.**
    a. hostages   b. rebellion   c. treason

_____ **7.** The Civil War began when states **separated** from the United States.
    a. seceded   b. captured   c. admitted

A Second Look at Vocabulary

Complete the sentences. Use the words in the box.

abolitionists	arsenal	issue	secede
acres	hostages	rebellion	treason

1. John Brown was found guilty of _____.

2. The army stored gunpowder and other explosives in the _____.

3. Taxes are an important _____ in many elections.

4. The American Revolution was a _____ against Great Britain.

5. The Union believed that states had no right to _____.

6. How many _____ did John Brown capture at Harpers Ferry?

7. The _____ wanted to end slavery forever.

8. Some people in Virginia owned thousands of _____ of land.

West Virginia

Understanding the Reading

Choose the best answer.

_____ 1. Many people in western Virginia owned
  a. small farms or no land at all.
  b. many slaves.
  c. large plantations.

_____ 2. John Brown attacked the arsenal at Harpers Ferry because he
  a. wanted to start his own country.
  b. wanted to start a slave rebellion.
  c. believed that the southern states would secede.

_____ 3. When Virginia seceded, people of western Virginia
  a. joined the rebellion.
  b. became abolitionists.
  c. voted to form their own state.

Fact or Opinion?

Mark each statement _F_ for _fact_ or _O_ for _opinion_.

_____ 1. The landowners of eastern Virginia wanted to control the state.

_____ 2. John Brown was wrong in attacking the U.S. arsenal.

_____ 3. The abolitionists believed all slaves should be freed.

_____ 4. John Brown should not have been hanged for treason.

When Did It Happen?

Write numbers to put the events in the order they happened.

_____ Abraham Lincoln was elected president.

_____ John Brown attacked the arsenal.

_____ West Virginia became the 35th state.

_____ War broke out between the Confederate and Union troops.

What Do You Think?
Discuss these questions.

1. Why did John Brown want to start a slave rebellion? Was violence the only way to end slavery?

2. Should people break the law if they disagree with the government?

3. How do you think the people of West Virginia feel about their history? Why?

A Last Look
Write about one of these topics.

1. Learn more about John Brown. Is he a hero? Why or why not?

2. Virginia gave voting rights only to white men who owned more than 25 acres of land. Look up voting rights in early America. Why was owning land important for voting?

Southeast Region

Alabama, Arkansas, Florida, Georgia, Kentucky, Louisiana, Mississippi, North Carolina, South Carolina, Tennessee

A Quick Look at this Region

The first European settlers in the Southeast were English, Spanish, and French. The region had long, warm summers and short, mild winters. Its rich soil and ample rain were good for crops. By the 1700s, large plantations grew tobacco, cotton, rice, and sugar cane. The region became the country's farming center. Plantation owners brought slaves from Africa to work in the fields.

Slavery was an important issue in the Civil War of 1861–1865. All of the states in this region except Kentucky left the Union to join the Confederacy. After the South was defeated, slavery was ended. In the South, however, the free black Americans were denied many rights. The civil rights movement of the 1950s and 1960s struggled to gain those rights.

Since World War II, the population of this region has grown rapidly. Businesses provide services such as banking and communications. Others make furniture, chemicals, and soft drinks. Farms grow fruits, vegetables, and grain along with cotton and tobacco. Tourists come to see the Blue Ridge, Great Smoky, and Ozark mountains. Others enjoy the ocean and beaches.

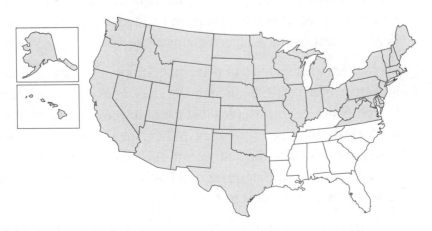

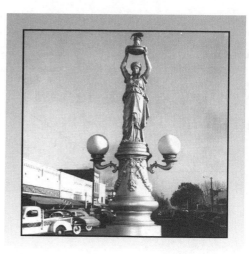

Alabama

Thinking about the Picture

1. This statue is a woman holding a giant insect. Why would people build this statue?
2. What other monuments have you seen?

King Cotton

Early settlers in Alabama began to grow cotton in the late 1700s. It soon became the state's most important agricultural product. Growing and processing cotton was hard work. It took a whole day for a worker to take the seeds out of just one pound of cotton. In 1793, the cotton gin was introduced. Eli Whitney patented the machine, but others had similar ideas. The gin took seeds quickly out of picked cotton. With a cotton gin, a worker could process 50 times as much cotton in a day.

Thousands of people moved to Alabama to grow cotton. They set up large farms called plantations. For plantation owners, cotton was "white gold." By the 1840s and 1850s, people called the crop "King Cotton." But growing cotton depended on the work of slaves. They had to plant and pick cotton in the hot sun. With the cotton gin, farms could process more cotton faster. That meant more slaves were needed.

After the Civil War ended in 1865, cotton continued as Alabama's main crop. Farmers planted it year after year. They did not plant other crops to give the soil a rest. By the 1880s, the land was worn out. To make things worse, an insect called the Mexican boll weevil reached the state in 1915. It began to destroy the Alabama cotton crop.

Alabama farmers had to plant other crops. They started planting peanuts and other food crops. Soon many farmers were making more money than before. Some people decided that the boll weevil was actually a blessing. It made them introduce new crops. In fact, the people of Enterprise, Alabama, built a monument to the boll weevil. It is probably the only monument in the world to a pest. Enterprise now has one of the largest peanut butter factories in the United States.

Today cotton is still the state's leading crop. Soybeans, peanuts, peaches, and other food crops are also important.

Alabama

A First Look at Vocabulary

Match each term with its meaning.

_____ 1. agricultural   a. used until no longer useful

_____ 2. blessing   b. needed

_____ 3. depended   c. animal that does damage

_____ 4. monument   d. dirt; ground

_____ 5. pest   e. statue or building that reminds people of something

_____ 6. process   f. related to farming

_____ 7. soil   g. prepare for use

_____ 8. worn out   h. favor from God

A Second Look at Vocabulary

Complete the story. Use the words in the box.

agricultural	depended	pest	soil
blessing	monument	processing	worn out

Cotton was an important _____ product in Alabama. However,
1

_____ cotton by removing the seeds took much time. Plantation
2

owners _____ on slaves to do this work.
3

Cotton was the only crop grown on some of the land. In time, the

_____ would no longer grow healthy cotton. The land was
4

_____. Then an insect _____ attacked the
5   6

cotton. Farmers tried to raise peanuts and other crops. They made more money than

before. They decided the boll weevil had been a _____. They even
7

built a _____ to the insect.
8

Understanding the Reading

Choose the best answer.

_____ 1. The cotton gin made it easier to
   a. pick cotton.
   b. plant cotton.
   c. take seeds out of cotton.

_____ 2. Because of the cotton gin,
   a. more slaves were needed for planting cotton.
   b. farmers began growing other crops.
   c. plantations did not grow enough cotton.

_____ 3. The farmers in Alabama wore out the soil by
   a. planting different crops each year.
   b. planting only cotton year after year.
   c. not planting anything for a few years.

_____ 4. Farmers started planting peanuts, soybeans, and other crops because
   a. people bought less cotton.
   b. they didn't have enough slaves.
   c. the boll weevils ate up their cotton plants.

_____ 5. Today, the biggest crop in Alabama is
   a. cotton.
   b. peanuts.
   c. soybeans.

When Did It Happen?

Write numbers to put the events in the order they happened.

_____ Alabama farmers began to grow peanuts, soybeans, and other crops.

_____ People began to call cotton "King Cotton."

_____ Enterprise, Alabama, built a monument to the boll weevil.

_____ Cotton became the most important crop in Alabama.

_____ Boll weevils ate up the cotton crop.

What Do You Think?
Discuss these questions.

1. Do you like cotton clothing? Why or why not?
2. The cotton gin made a big change in Alabama. What are some other inventions that have made a big difference in people's lives?

A Last Look
Write about one of these topics.

1. Write about a time in your life when something that seemed bad was really a blessing.
2. Look up one of Alabama's other crops, such as peanuts or soybeans. What products are made from these crops? Do you use any of them?

Alabama

Arkansas

Thinking about the Picture

1. Why do people enjoy soaking in hot water?
2. Have you ever visited a hot spring or spa? Describe your experience.

Hot Springs

When water from underground flows out of cracks in the rock, it creates a spring. Springs bring water to lakes and streams. Most spring water is cool. In some places, though, the water flows past hot underground rock. It comes to the surface as a steaming hot spring. Hot springs are found in only a few places in the United States. One is Hot Springs, Arkansas. Hot Springs National Park has 47 thermal springs. The average water temperature is 143°F (62°C).

For centuries, people have believed that hot springs are healthful. The waters contain minerals. Both the warmth and the minerals may help physical problems. Native Americans in Arkansas knew about the springs. They used the waters to cure illnesses. They thought of the springs as a holy place. In 1541, the Spanish explorer Hernando de Soto reached Arkansas. He was probably the first European to see the hot springs.

In the 1800s, French and Spanish settlers discovered the Arkansas hot springs. The waters helped ease pains such as arthritis. The news spread, and the area became a health center. In 1832, the federal government made the hot springs a protected area. In 1921, they became a national park.

From the late 1800s until the 1920s, many grand hotels and bathhouses were built in Hot Springs. They were elegant buildings, with marble pools and tubs. They offered thermal baths and healing massages. Movie stars, athletes, and presidents came there. An Army-Navy Hospital opened in Hot Springs in 1887. Injured soldiers were sent there for treatment.

After the 1940s, competition and medical advances hurt Hot Springs. Many bathhouses closed. Today, eight buildings on "Bathhouse Row" are historic landmarks. The Fordyce Bathhouse was restored in 1989 to show what the "Golden Age" of Hot Springs was like. It is the visitor center for the national park. Other hotels still offer spa treatments.

A First Look at Vocabulary

Choose the word that matches each definition in bold type.

_____ 1. The **flow of water from the ground** was clear and cold.

       a. minerals   b. bath   c. spring

_____ 2. The **hot** water came from deep in the ground.

       a. thermal   b. spring   c. massage

_____ 3. Many people believe that spring water is **good for the body.**

       a. restful   b. healthful   c. youthful

_____ 4. Disease and pain are problems **of the body.**

       a. physical   b. elegant   c. average

_____ 5. Can hot water **make someone recover from** a disease?

       a. protect   b. prevent   c. cure

_____ 6. People will try anything to **lessen** their pain.

       a. fix   b. cure   c. ease

_____ 7. The bathhouses were **graceful.**

       a. elegant   b. strong   c. old

_____ 8. After a bath, a **rubbing** on the body takes away pain.

       a. medical advance   b. treatment   c. massage

A Second Look at Vocabulary

Complete the sentences. Use the words from the box.

cure	elegant	springs
eased	massage	thermal

1. I felt better, but the hot spring did not _____ my injured hand.

2. The _____ bathhouse was beautifully built.

3. A _____ may make a backache go away.

4. Water from the _____ spring is too hot to touch.

5. Some _____ have very hot water while others have cold water.

6. Hot water _____ the pain in my shoulder.

Arkansas

Understanding the Reading

Choose the best answer.

_____ 1. The water in the Arkansas springs is made hot when it
   a. is heated at the bathhouses.
   b. flows past hot underground rocks.
   c. is warmed by the sun.

_____ 2. Hotels and bathhouses
   a. are no longer at Hot Springs.
   b. were never popular and soon closed.
   c. were built from the late 1800s to the 1920s.

_____ 3. The hot springs in Arkansas are
   a. protected as a national park.
   b. no longer in use.
   c. used only by Native Americans.

Fact or Opinion?

Mark each statement _F_ for _fact_ or _O_ for _opinion_.

_____ 1. The average temperature of the springs is 143°F.

_____ 2. Native Americans thought the springs were a holy place.

_____ 3. People were foolish to think the hot springs cured disease.

_____ 4. There are only a few places where hot springs are found.

_____ 5. The government should protect the Fordyce Bathhouse.

When Did It Happen?

Write numbers to put the events in the order they happened.

_____ Hernando de Soto visited the hot springs.

_____ The United States made the hot springs a national park.

_____ Hotels and bathhouses were built at the springs.

_____ French and Spanish settlers came to the springs to ease health problems.

What Do You Think?

Discuss these questions.

1. Why do some people believe a hot spring is a holy place? Why do they think it can cure disease or ease pain? Do you agree?

2. Protecting the hot springs as a national park costs money. So does restoring the Fordyce Bathhouse. Is this a good use of tax money? Why or why not?

A Last Look

Write about one of these topics.

1. Learn about another place in the United States that has hot springs. How are those springs used?

2. Find out what happens when people go to a bathhouse in Hot Springs. How are they treated? What is done for them?

Florida

Thinking about the Picture

1. What kind of ride is this? Why do people enjoy parks that have these types of rides?
2. Who goes to these parks?

Theme Parks

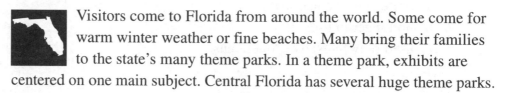

Visitors come to Florida from around the world. Some come for warm winter weather or fine beaches. Many bring their families to the state's many theme parks. In a theme park, exhibits are centered on one main subject. Central Florida has several huge theme parks.

Perhaps the most famous park is Walt Disney World near Orlando. It opened in 1971. Its theme was the cartoon characters invented by Walt Disney. Now Disney World is four separate parks. They are the Magic Kingdom, Epcot Center, Disney-MGM Studios, and Disney's Animal Kingdom. Visitors to the Magic Kingdom meet famous Disney characters such as Mickey Mouse. They visit a Wild West town and see old-fashioned American scenes. Other exhibits show life around the world.

Epcot Center has two main sections. The theme of Future World is technology that may be part of the future. One exhibit is a huge geosphere called "Spaceship Earth." World Showcase presents cultures of other countries. The exhibits at Disney-MGM Studios give visitors a history of the movies. Disney's Animal Kingdom is the newest section. It features both real and imaginary animals.

Universal Studios Theme Park is also two separate parks. The theme of Universal Studios/Florida is movie making. Visitors can tour the sets for movies and TV shows. Exhibits are based on some of the studio's most popular movies. Islands of Adventure is the other theme park. Its adventure tours are based on favorite books and movies.

Sea World lives up to its name. Its theme is sea creatures—marine mammals, fish, birds, and reptiles. It is famous for its animal shows. Whales, dolphins, and seals perform. Visitors can swim with dolphins or go snorkeling with tropical fish.

Florida

A First Look at Vocabulary

Match each term with its meaning.

_____ **1.** theme park   a. go around looking at things

_____ **2.** exhibit   b. person or animal in a story

_____ **3.** cartoon   c. connected to the ocean or sea

_____ **4.** character   d. something that is shown to people

_____ **5.** old-fashioned   e. park with entertainment about a main subject

_____ **6.** technology   f. do things to entertain

_____ **7.** features   g. has as a main idea

_____ **8.** tour   h. a funny drawing of a person, animal, or thing

_____ **9.** marine   i. things produced by science and industry

_____ **10.** perform   j. like things were in the past

A Second Look at Vocabulary

Complete the sentences. Use the words from the first exercise.

1. A _____ exhibit has animals that live in the ocean.

2. Birds _____ tricks at the bird exhibit.

3. Fast rides, fun characters, and other entertainment are found at a _____.

4. If a _____ from a cartoon waves to you, say hello.

5. If an exhibit _____ animals of Africa, look for lions and elephants.

6. Mickey Mouse or another character from a _____ might walk up to you.

7. People who work in a history theme park wear _____ clothing.

8. Some exhibits show the latest _____ like scientific advances and new products from industry.

9. _____ the park to see all the different exhibits.

10. You might see an _____ about the jungle or climbing a mountain.

Understanding the Reading

Choose the best answer.

_____ 1. Visitors mainly come to Florida to visit
    a. movie studios and large cities.
    b. theme parks and mountains.
    c. theme parks and beaches.

_____ 2. When Walt Disney World was started, its theme was
    a. Walt Disney's cartoon characters.
    b. the history of movies.
    c. technology of the future.

_____ 3. Epcot Center
    a. gives visitors a tour of islands of the world.
    b. helps visitors learn about sea creatures.
    c. is part of Disney World.

Fact or Opinion?

Mark each statement _F_ for _fact_ or _O_ for _opinion_.

_____ 1. Florida has the best theme parks in the United States.

_____ 2. Walt Disney World opened in 1971.

_____ 3. Epcot Center is more fun than the Magic Kingdom.

_____ 4. Florida's theme parks are educational and entertaining.

What Do You Think?

Discuss these questions.

1. Why do you think people around the world love the Disney cartoon characters?
2. Why do people want to know what life will be like in the future?

A Last Look

Write about one of these topics.

1. Which Florida theme park would you like to visit? Why?
2. Some people say theme parks are not good and just make money for their owners. Do you agree or disagree? Why?

Alike or Different?

Complete the chart to compare and contrast the theme parks. The first row is done as an example.

Name of Park	Theme	What Visitors Do
Disney-MGM Studios	Movies	Learn about history of movies
Magic Kingdom		
Universal Studios/Florida		
Sea World		

Georgia

Thinking about the Picture

1. Who was Martin Luther King, Jr.?
2. Why is it important to remember people like Dr. King?

Dr. Martin Luther King, Jr.

Atlanta, Georgia, was the home of the most famous leader of the civil rights movement. Martin Luther King, Jr., was born there on January 15, 1929. King went to Morehouse College and then to graduate school. He became a minister like his father. Besides Christian teachings, King followed the nonviolent ideas of Mohandas Gandhi.

When King was growing up, racial segregation was common. After the Civil War, amendments to the U.S. Constitution guaranteed the civil rights of African Americans. In real life, they did not have those rights. In the South, segregation was often the law. In the North, it had other causes. Blacks and whites often went to separate schools. Restrooms, theaters, and lunch counters were segregated. In the South, so were trains and buses.

In the 1950s and 1960s, the civil rights movement got stronger. By then King was pastor of a church in Montgomery, Alabama. In 1955, he led a protest against the city's segregated bus system. King taught his followers to be nonviolent. They marched and sang. They "sat in" at lunch counters. Angry whites sometimes attacked them. But the fight went on.

In 1963, civil rights leaders organized a march to the Lincoln Memorial in Washington, D.C. More than 200,000 people heard Martin Luther King make a powerful speech. It was called "I Have a Dream." His dream, King said, was that people would be judged by their character, not the color of their skins. In 1964, Congress passed a strong civil rights bill. It banned discrimination in all public places. That year King received the Nobel Peace Prize for his work. In 1965, Congress passed the Voting Rights Act.

Many people admired King. Others hated and feared him. On April 4, 1968, he was shot and killed in Memphis, Tennessee. He was buried in Atlanta. Today a national holiday in January celebrates his life.

A First Look at Vocabulary

Choose the best definition for each word in bold type.

_____ 1. The U.S. Constitution protects **civil rights.**
   a. legal rights   b. special privileges   c. private opinions

_____ 2. Martin Luther King, Jr., was a leader of the civil rights **movement.**
   a. confused action   b. lack of action   c. organized action

_____ 3. King believed that **nonviolent** actions would succeed.
   a. that doesn't hurt   b. that doesn't help   c. that doesn't speak

_____ 4. Some states allowed **segregated** schools.
   a. free   b. separate   c. private

_____ 5. The U.S. Constitution has had 26 **amendments.**
   a. changes   b. sections   c. elections

_____ 6. Many people joined **protests** to speak out against unfair conditions.
   a. private talks   b. votes   c. acts of disagreeing

_____ 7. Members of the Senate voted on a **bill.**
   a. suggested law   b. approved law   c. change to the Constitution

_____ 8. Denying people jobs because of their race is **discrimination.**
   a. unequal treatment   b. fair treatment   c. legal treatment

A Second Look at Vocabulary

Complete the story. Use the words from the first exercise.

The Constitution and its _____ promise _____
                                    1   2
to all people. But African Americans lived with _____. Some places
                                                          3
allowed _____ schools and other unjust conditions.
                    4

Many people wanted to change the country. Dr. Martin Luther King, Jr., was one

leader of this _____. He led _____ in which people
                        5   6
disagreed with the government. All of these actions were _____.
                                                                      7
Many protestors got hurt, but they didn't try to hurt anyone else. Finally Congress

listened. A _____ was passed to protect civil rights.
                      8

Understanding the Reading

Choose the best answer.

_____ **1.** After the Civil War, the U.S. Constitution was changed to give civil rights to African Americans,
   a. but they did not get those rights.
   b. but Dr. King wanted more segregation.
   c. and the civil rights movement ended.

_____ **2.** Dr. King wanted his followers to
   a. use nonviolence during protests.
   b. use violence when needed.
   c. stop protesting.

_____ **3.** During a march in Washington, D.C., Dr. King
   a. was shot and killed.
   b. was given the Nobel Peace Prize.
   c. gave a speech called "I Have a Dream."

Reading between the Lines

Look carefully at the reading. Mark each statement _T_ for _true_ or _F_ for _false_.

_____ **1.** Dr. King's use of nonviolent protests was not successful.

_____ **2.** Protesting for civil rights was dangerous.

_____ **3.** Dr. King said that discrimination because of skin color was wrong.

_____ **4.** Southern states said that segregation was the law.

When Did It Happen?

Write numbers to put the events in the order they happened.

_____ Dr. King gave a speech called "I Have a Dream."

_____ Congress passed the Civil Rights Bill.

_____ Dr. King led the protest against the segregated bus system in Montgomery, Alabama.

_____ Congress passed the Voting Rights Act.

What Do You Think?
Discuss these questions.

1. Why do you suppose Dr. King used only nonviolent methods to try to win civil rights?
2. Why did white people as well as African Americans join the civil rights movement?

A Last Look
Write about one of these topics.

1. Tell about a great leader who changed life in your native country. What did this leader do?
2. Is the struggle for civil rights over? Have all of Dr. King's goals been reached?

Kentucky

Thinking about the Picture
1. What is this rider doing? How do you know?
2. Why do people enjoy watching horse races?
3. Have you been to any kind of race? Describe it.

Kentucky Derby

 The Kentucky Derby is the most famous horse race in the United States. It is run yearly in Louisville, Kentucky, on the first Saturday in May. The Derby is also America's oldest horse race. It began in 1875. It takes only about two minutes for the horses to finish the race. It is called "the most exciting two minutes in sports."

Not everyone watches the race on TV, though. Every year about 130,000 people crowd into the stands. The Kentucky Derby is run at Churchill Downs, a 180-acre park. The oval racetrack is $1\frac{1}{4}$ miles (about 2,000 meters) long. The race is for 3-year-old horses.

Horse racing is a Kentucky tradition. In 1775, Kentucky farms began to raise horses called Thoroughbreds. To be a Thoroughbred, a horse must be descended from one of three famous Arabian horses. Those horses were brought to England in the late 1600s and early 1700s. Arabian horses were famous for their speed. Only Thoroughbreds run in the Derby.

The history of the Kentucky Derby began with Colonel M. Lewis Clark. In the early 1870s, Clark studied horse racing in France and England. When he came home to Kentucky, he decided to start horse races in Louisville. It would be a way for Kentucky horse farms to show off their best horses.

In 1874, Clark started the Louisville Jockey Club. The land belonged to his uncles, John and Henry Churchill. Clark built a clubhouse, a track, six stables, and a grandstand for spectators. The first race was held in 1875. He modeled it on a race in England called the Epsom Derby. By 1883, a Louisville newspaper called the park "Churchill Downs."

Another Derby tradition began in the 1890s. A blanket of roses was placed on the neck of the winning horse. In 1925, a New York sportswriter called the Derby "the Run for the Roses." It has had that nickname ever since.

Kentucky

A First Look at Vocabulary

Choose the best definition for each word in bold type.

_____ **1.** The Kentucky Derby is a **famous** horse race.

    a. old   b. costly   c. well-known

_____ **2.** If you don't want to **crowd** into the park, don't go to the race.

    a. sneak   b. push   c. hurry

_____ **3.** The **stands** are full of excited people.

    a. hallways   b. entrances   c. seats

_____ **4.** The racetrack at Churchill Downs is **oval.**

    a. shaped like an egg   b. shaped like a box   c. shaped like a ball

_____ **5.** Horse racing in Kentucky has many **traditions.**

    a. animals   b. old customs   c. difficulties

_____ **6.** Six horses were kept in the **stable.**

    a. farmland   b. racetrack   c. shelter for horses

_____ **7.** **Spectators** at the Kentucky Derby often travel far to see the race.

    a. people who watch   b. people who listen   c. people who ride

_____ **8.** Do you like the **nickname** "the Run for the Roses"?

    a. funny name   b. informal name   c. legal name

A Second Look at Vocabulary

Complete the sentences. Use the words from the first exercise.

1. An _____ racetrack is more sensible than a square one.

2. The horses rest and are fed in the _____.

3. Besides the _____ in the stands, millions more watch the race on TV.

4. "The Kentucky Derby" is the real name of the race, not a _____.

5. The _____ of the Kentucky Derby remind people of its long history.

6. The horse became _____ when it won the Kentucky Derby.

7. On Derby day, there is not an empty seat left in the _____.

8. Thousands of people _____ through the doors and hurry to find their seats.

Understanding the Reading

Choose the best answer.

_____ 1. The most famous horse race in the United States is the
   a. Kentucky Derby.
   b. Epsom Derby.
   c. Churchill Downs.

_____ 2. The Kentucky Derby is for
   a. 2-year-old horses.
   b. 3-year-old horses.
   c. 5-year-old horses.

_____ 3. All Thoroughbreds are descended from
   a. Colonel M. Lewis Clark's horses.
   b. horses from France and England.
   c. one of three Arabian horses.

_____ 4. Clark learned about horse racing
   a. from his uncles, John and Henry Churchill.
   b. at the Louisville Jockey Club.
   c. by studying horse racing in France and England.

_____ 5. A sports writer called the Kentucky Derby " the Run for the Roses" because the
   a. winner gets to the rose garden first.
   b. winning horse is given a blanket of roses.
   c. first winning horse was called "Rose."

When Did It Happen?

Write numbers to put the events in the order they happened.

_____ Clark started the Louisville Jockey Club.

_____ The Kentucky Derby started.

_____ A sportswriter called the Derby "the Run for the Roses."

_____ Kentucky farms began to raise Thoroughbreds.

_____ Clark studied horse racing in England and France.

_____ The winning horse was given a blanket of roses.

What Do You Think?
Discuss these questions.

1. Why do you think horse racing is so popular?

2. Many people think horses are beautiful animals. What is beautiful about horses?

3. Would you like to work with racehorses? Why or why not?

A Last Look
Write about one of these topics.

1. The Kentucky Derby is the first race in the "Triple Crown." What are the other races? How are they different? Why are they called the Triple Crown?

2. Find out about one famous horse that won the Kentucky Derby. Describe the horse's career.

3. Learn about Kentucky horse farms. What makes them good for raising horses? Do the best horses all come from Kentucky?

Kentucky

Louisiana

Thinking about the Picture

1. What instrument is this musician playing?

2. What are some different kinds of music?

3. How is jazz different from other kinds of music?

New Orleans, Cradle of Jazz

 Jazz is America's own music. Traditional jazz began in New Orleans, Louisiana, in the late 1800s. Like the city of New Orleans, jazz is a mix of many cultures.

At first, Louisiana was a colony of France. It passed to Spain in 1762, then back to France. In 1803 the United States bought the Louisiana Territory. New Orleans was a colorful mix of cultures—Creole, African, West Indian. Creoles were the descendants of French and Spanish settlers. The city had thousands of enslaved African Americans. Their ancestors came from West Africa. There were also many free "persons of color." Some were blacks from the West Indies. Others were of mixed ancestry. The traditions of all these people influenced jazz.

In New Orleans, slaves were allowed to get together in public. They played West African music and sang work songs and "spirituals." Later, the black community built a tradition of band music for funerals and parades. On the way to funerals, the music was slow and sad. On the way back, they played lively songs. In the late 1890s, white people hired black marching bands for their celebrations. Two other new musical styles also influenced jazz. One was "ragtime." The other was the blues.

By 1900, black New Orleans musicians were playing "traditional" jazz in the dance halls of Storyville. The city produced many great jazz musicians. One was Louis Armstrong, a trumpet player with a hoarse singing voice. Another was a pianist, Jelly Roll Morton. Whites soon learned this new music. In 1917, white musicians from New Orleans formed the "Original Dixieland Jazz Band." They made the first jazz recording.

In 1968, New Orleans held its first Jazz and Heritage Festival. Today jazz lovers from around the world travel to New Orleans to enjoy this unique American style.

A First Look at Vocabulary

Match each term with its meaning.

_____ **1.** jazz   a. groups marching together to celebrate something

_____ **2.** colorful   b. ceremony to honor a person who has died

_____ **3.** ancestors   c. person who plays or sings music

_____ **4.** influenced   d. very interesting

_____ **5.** spirituals   e. only one of its type

_____ **6.** band   f. a type of music invented by African Americans

_____ **7.** funeral   g. group of people playing musical instruments

_____ **8.** parade   h. relatives from the past

_____ **9.** musician   i. African American religious songs

_____ **10.** unique   j. affected; changed

A Second Look at Vocabulary

Complete the sentences. Use the words from the first exercise.

1. Louis Armstrong was a great jazz _____.

2. A band played spirituals at the _____ of a man who died two days before.

3. Many musicians live _____ lives, so it is interesting to learn about them.

4. The _____ of African American slaves lived in Africa.

5. _____ is a truly American type of music.

6. Jazz musicians change songs when they play, so each performance is _____.

7. Jazz has _____ many other kinds of rock music.

8. People sang _____ in church and when they worked and played, too.

9. Several bands marched in the _____ down Main Street.

10. The _____ had a trumpet player, a violinist, and a drummer.

Louisiana

Understanding the Reading

Choose the best answer.

_____ **1.** Jazz
- a. started in New Orleans.
- b. was brought to America by African slaves.
- c. was first played at funerals.

_____ **2.** When the United States bought the Louisiana Territory,
- a. most people there were French or Spanish.
- b. it had a mix of many cultures.
- c. slavery was against the law.

_____ **3.** One reason that jazz began in New Orleans is because
- a. slaves were allowed to get together in public.
- b. slaves were allowed to buy musical instruments.
- c. slaves were encouraged to perform at funerals.

_____ **4.** Jazz was influenced by spirituals, work songs, ragtime, and
- a. rap.
- b. rock and roll.
- c. blues.

_____ **5.** The first jazz recording was made by
- a. Louis Armstrong.
- b. the Original Dixieland Jazz Band.
- c. Jelly Roll Morton.

Where's the Idea?

These are main ideas from the reading. Write the number of the paragraph where you find each idea.

_____ Black musicians developed traditional jazz, and soon it was spreading through America.

_____ When the United States purchased Louisiana, it had a mix of people from many cultures.

_____ People come from around the world to listen to jazz in New Orleans.

_____ Jazz is a unique American music.

_____ Jazz developed from the music and culture of slaves.

What Do You Think?
Discuss these questions.

1. What is your favorite type of music? Why do you like it?

2. Do you think jazz could have developed somewhere else? Why or why not?

A Last Look
Write about one of these topics.

1. Look up the life of Louis Armstrong, Jelly Roll Morton, Scott Joplin, Miles Davis, or another jazz musician. Write a summary of this person's life.

2. Listen to a jazz recording. Describe it. What do you like about it? Is there anything you don't like about it?

Mississippi

Thinking about the Picture

1. How were African Americans treated in the 20th century?
2. What might an African American writer write about? Why?

Richard Wright

Richard Wright was one of the first African American writers to express anger at how blacks were treated in the U.S. Wright's powerful style made him a major American writer. He had a strong influence on later African American writers.

Wright was born in 1908 near Natchez, Mississippi. His grandparents had been slaves. His father was a poor sharecropper. In about 1913, the family moved to Memphis, Tennessee, and his father abandoned them. His mother took Richard and his brother to live with relatives in Arkansas. While they were there, Richard's uncle was murdered by white men. Then his mother became ill, and Richard went to his grandparents in Jackson, Mississippi.

The hatred and fear between black and white Americans made Wright unhappy. In 1927, he moved north to Chicago. He hoped to escape prejudice, but he found it everywhere. He worked at several jobs, then began to write. He then went to New York. In 1938, Wright won a prize for a collection of short novels, called *Uncle Tom's Children*. It showed the prejudice that black Americans faced in Mississippi.

Two years later, Wright wrote a novel called *Native Son*. It became a best seller. *Native Son* is the story of a young black American in Chicago. He accidentally kills a white woman and is put to death for the crime. During his trial, he finally understands that society is against him.

In 1945, Wright wrote *Black Boy*. In it, he looked back at his childhood in the South. He described how African Americans were forced to accept discrimination. *Black Boy* showed black Americans trying to keep self-respect in spite of their situation.

Wright grew tired of the prejudice in the United States. He moved to Paris, France, in 1946. He lived in Europe until he died in 1960.

A First Look at Vocabulary

Match each term with its meaning.

_____ **1.** express   a. left behind

_____ **2.** pain   b. met a problem

_____ **3.** abandoned   c. disgusted by; no longer interested in

_____ **4.** prejudice   d. long work of fiction

_____ **5.** prize   e. talk about; describe

_____ **6.** faced   f. mental or physical suffering

_____ **7.** novel   g. feeling good about oneself

_____ **8.** society   h. award

_____ **9.** self-respect   i. unfair feelings about certain people

_____ **10.** tired of   j. group of people who share customs, laws, and history

A Second Look at Vocabulary

Complete the sentences. Use the words from the first exercise.

1. Richard Wright hated the _____ that many white Americans showed toward African Americans.

2. Richard Wright _____ discrimination in Chicago just as in Mississippi.

3. Native Son is a _____ about a young African American in Chicago.

4. Wright moved to Paris because he was _____ the prejudice in America.

5. Wright's books show the _____ caused by prejudice.

6. Wright's father _____ his family, so Wright grew up without a father.

7. Wright's novels _____ his anger and the love he felt in his family.

8. It is hard to keep your _____ when other people treat you badly.

9. Wright was angry about the prejudice he saw in American _____.

10. Some writers become popular after they win a _____ for their writing.

Understanding the Reading

Choose the best answer.

_____ **1.** In his books, Wright describes
     a. the freedom from prejudice he found in Chicago.
     b. the history of prejudice in America.
     c. the pain of being an African American.

_____ **2.** After Wright's father abandoned them, Wright's mother took the family
     a. to live with relatives.
     b. to Chicago.
     c. to Natchez.

_____ **3.** *Native Son* is different from Wright's other books because
     a. it tells about African Americans outside the South.
     b. it tells about African Americans in the South.
     c. it is not about African Americans.

_____ **4.** In *Black Boy*, Wright describes how black Americans were forced
     a. to live on farms in the South.
     b. to accept discrimination.
     c. give up their self-respect.

Why Did It Happen?

Match the sentence parts.

_____ **1.** Wright went to live with his grandparents

_____ **2.** Wright was one of America's major writers

_____ **3.** Wright was unhappy in America

_____ **4.** Wright moved to Paris

a. so he had a great influence on later writers.

b. because he wanted to get away from prejudice in America.

c. because his mother became sick.

d. because of the hatred and fear between white and black Americans.

What Do You Think?

Discuss these questions.

1. Why are people prejudiced? What can be done to reduce prejudice?

2. How can a writer change society?

3. Have conditions for African Americans become better since Richard Wright was writing? Give reasons to support your answer.

A Last Look

Write about one of these topics.

1. Learn about another modern African American writer, such as James Baldwin, Zora Neale Hurston, or Toni Morrison. Write a short biography of the writer.

2. If you were a writer, what social problem would you choose to write about? Why?

Mississippi

North Carolina

Thinking about the Picture

1. How is this airplane like those of today? How is it different?
2. What makes an airplane fly?
3. What skills would someone need to invent an airplane?

The Wright Brothers

In December 1903, a tiny one-man airplane flew over the sand dunes near Kitty Hawk, North Carolina. Wilbur Wright and his brother Orville had built the first successful airplane.

Wilbur Wright was born in Indiana in 1867. His family moved to Ohio, where Orville was born in 1871. Both the brothers were clever and skillful with machinery. They established a successful business designing and making bicycles. In the 1890s, other inventors were experimenting with flight and engines. Wilbur began to read about experiments with gliders. These are light airplanes that have no motors but are carried by the wind. Orville also got interested. Soon the brothers were studying everything known about flight. In 1899, they built their first glider.

The North Carolina coast has strong, steady winds. Between 1900 and 1902, the Wrights tested gliders there. These flights helped them improve the design. They learned how to control the planes. Next, they turned to powered flights—using an engine.

The brothers made a light aluminum engine for their glider. They returned to Kitty Hawk. On December 17, Wilbur took off in *Flyer I*. He kept the plane in the air for 12 seconds. It was the first flight of a powered and controlled airplane. Two years later the Wrights built the first practical airplane.

The Wright brothers were afraid that someone might steal their ideas. They tried to interest the government in their invention, but no one believed them. For several years, the brothers worked in secret. They improved their airplanes and engines. In 1908, the U.S. Army finally agreed to build an airplane. The Wrights began to give public demonstrations. Crowds of people watched in amazement. They began to understand the importance of this invention.

Wilbur Wright died in 1912. Orville lived until 1948. Their first plane is in the National Air and Space Museum in Washington, D.C.

A First Look at Vocabulary

Choose the best definition for each word in bold type.

_____ 1. The **pilot** flew the airplane along the coast.
    a. flier   b. builder   c. designer

_____ 2. Someone must be very **clever** to invent an airplane.
    a. strong   b. smart   c. educated

_____ 3. The Wright brothers **established** a bicycle business.
    a. sold   b. bought   c. set up

_____ 4. The **glider** was held up by a strong wind.
    a. bicycle   b. aircraft   c. automobile

_____ 5. They kept improving the **design** of their first airplane.
    a. plan   b. picture   c. flight

_____ 6. The **engine** was made of aluminum, so it was light.
    a. motor   b. wing   c. design

_____ 7. Did anyone **steal** the design from the Wright brothers?
    a. borrow   b. buy   c. take

_____ 8. The **demonstration** proved that flight was practical.
    a. show   b. dream   c. design

A Second Look at Vocabulary

Complete the sentences. Use the words from the first exercise.

1. It's wrong to _____ things or ideas.

2. My father can solve many puzzles. He is very _____.

3. I will build a chair if I can find a good _____.

4. A flying squirrel soars like a _____. It doesn't fly like a bird.

5. The brothers _____ the fact that people could fly.

6. Do you know how to use this machine, or do you need a _____?

7. A _____ needs good training to fly safely.

8. The _____ in a car is bigger than the one in a motorcycle.

Understanding the Reading

Choose the best answer.

_____ **1.** Before the Wright brothers built airplanes, they established a business
     a. making automobiles and trucks.
     b. designing and building bicycles.
     c. building houses.

_____ **2.** The Wright brothers went to the North Carolina coast to fly their gliders because
     a. it was near their home.
     b. it has a beautiful beach.
     c. it has strong, steady winds.

_____ **3.** The first flight lasted just 12 seconds,
     a. and the brothers almost quit making planes.
     b. but it showed that flying was possible.
     c. so the brothers sold the design to the army.

Reading between the Lines

Look carefully at the reading. Mark each statement _T_ for _true_ or _F_ for _false_.

_____ **1.** The Wright brothers can be called "the Fathers of Aviation." (Aviation means flying.)

_____ **2.** The Wright brothers were the first to build gliders.

_____ **3.** At first, people didn't believe the brothers had flown.

_____ **4.** The army quickly agreed to buy the new airplane.

When Did It Happen?

Write numbers to put the events in the order they happened.

_____ The U.S. Army agreed to build an airplane.

_____ _Flyer I_ flew for 12 seconds at Kitty Hawk.

_____ The brothers gave public demonstrations of their airplane.

_____ The brothers built their first glider.

What Do You Think?
Discuss these questions.

1. Why did it take so long to learn to fly?
2. How has flying changed the world?
3. Some people love to fly. Others are afraid of it. Why do people have these different feelings?

A Last Look
Write about one of these topics.

1. Would you want to learn to fly? Why or why not?
2. Describe a flight that you have made. Did you enjoy it? What makes you remember it?

South Carolina

Thinking about the Picture

1. Mary McLeod Bethune was a well-known educator. Why is education important to people? Why is it important for society?
2. Why do some people spend their lives helping others?

Mary McLeod Bethune

 Mary McLeod Bethune spent her life working for the rights of other black Americans. She began her work in her home state of South Carolina. Mary Jane McLeod was born in 1875 in Mayesville, South Carolina. Her parents had been slaves. Like most African Americans in the South at the time, they were poor. As a child, Mary picked cotton. There were no schools for black children in Mayesville.

When McLeod was 11, a teacher named Emma Wilson came to the cotton fields. She was starting a new school for black Americans. Mary McLeod wanted very much to learn to read, so her parents sent her to school.

Mary McLeod was a talented student. A few years later, she received a scholarship. She studied at a religious school in Concord, North Carolina. Later she went to Moody Bible Institute in Chicago. She was the only African American student there. She became a teacher and went back to Mayesville. Later she taught in Augusta, Georgia, where she met Albertus Bethune. They were married in 1898 and moved to Florida. They had a son, but the couple separated.

Bethune believed that black Americans needed education to succeed. In 1904, she started a school for girls in Daytona, Florida. The school used wooden boxes for desks and charcoal for pencils. The local business community became interested in her dream. They gave money to support the school. In 1923, it became Bethune-Cookman College for men and women. Bethune was president of the college for 20 years.

In 1936, President Franklin Roosevelt appointed Bethune head of the Division for Negro Affairs. She was the first African American woman to run a federal agency. Bethune received many honors for her work. After President Roosevelt died, Eleanor Roosevelt gave Bethune his gold-headed cane. Bethune used it proudly until her death in 1955.

A First Look at Vocabulary

Match each term with its meaning.

_____ **1.** agency   a. partly burned wood

_____ **2.** appointed   b. given a job or position

_____ **3.** cane   c. part of the government

_____ **4.** charcoal   d. school that teaches a special subject

_____ **5.** institute   e. walking stick

_____ **6.** local   f. having natural ability

_____ **7.** poor   g. without much money

_____ **8.** scholarship   h. nearby

_____ **9.** support   i. money to pay for education

_____ **10.** talented   j. help

A Second Look at Vocabulary

Complete the story. Use the words from the first exercise.

Mary McLeod Bethune's parents were _____ , so she picked cotton

as a child. It helped her family pay for things they needed. When she went to school,

she did well. She was a _____ student. As a result, she got a

_____ to study at a religious school. Then she went to a Bible

_____ , where she learned to be a teacher.

She started a school for girls. It was a poor school. Students didn't have pencils.

They had to use _____ instead. Things got better when

_____ businesses gave some money to _____ the

school. It became a college in 1923.

A few years later, Bethune was _____ to a federal job. She became

head of an _____ of the federal government. Eleanor Roosevelt

respected Bethune. She gave her President Roosevelt's _____ .

Bethune used it to help her walk during the final years of her life.

Understanding the Reading

Choose the best answer.

_____ 1. As a young child, Mary McLeod did not go to school
   a. because the African American school was for boys only.
   b. because there were no schools for black children in her town.
   c. because her parents were too poor to send her.

_____ 2. McLeod studied at the Moody Bible Institute
   a. and became a teacher.
   b. and was asked to teach there.
   c. where she met and married Albertus Bethune.

_____ 3. In Florida, Bethune opened a school
   a. where she was the only African American.
   b. where she met Eleanor Roosevelt.
   c. that became Bethune-Cookman College.

_____ 4. As head of the Division of Negro Affairs, Bethune
   a. started the Moody Bible Institute for African Americans.
   b. was the first African American woman to run a federal agency.
   c. got money to support her school in Florida.

Why Did It Happen?

Match the sentence parts.

_____ 1. Mary wanted to learn to read,

_____ 2. Mrs. Roosevelt respected Bethune,

_____ 3. Local businesspeople thought education was important,

_____ 4. Bethune believed that black Americans needed education,

_____ 5. Mary McLeod's parents were poor,

   a. so she gave her President Roosevelt's cane.

   b. so her parents sent her to Emma Wilson's school.

   c. so she opened a school for black children.

   d. so she had to pick cotton.

   e. so they gave money to support Bethune's school.

Discuss these questions.

1. If you had to walk five miles to school, would you? Why or why not?
2. Why was it hard for black Americans to get an education when Mary McLeod was a child?
3. Why is Mary McLeod Bethune important in the history of the fight for equality for all people?

A Last Look

Write about one of these topics.

1. Learn about another African American who opened the way for others. You might look up Barbara Jordan, Ralph Bunche, or Thurgood Marshall, for example. What did this person do? Why is his or her success important?
2. Why do businesses often support education? What do they get from educated people? Besides giving money, what else can businesses do to support education?

South Carolina

Tennessee

Thinking about the Picture

1. What instruments do country music performers play?
2. What is country music? How is it different from other kinds of music?

Country Music

Nashville, Tennessee, is the center of the country music industry. Its nickname is *Music City, USA*.

The roots of country music were in the South. In the 1700s and 1800s, people from Great Britain settled in rural mountain areas. They brought familiar folk songs and fiddle tunes. They also heard the religious songs and the blues songs of black Americans. In the later 1800s, traveling shows brought popular music from New York to the South. Rural musicians began playing this music on their fiddles. They added guitars and banjos.

In 1924, a Chicago radio station broadcast a country music program. It was called the *National Barn Dance.* In 1925, a Nashville station started its own program. At first it was called the *WSM Barn Dance.* In 1927, it became the *Grand Ole Opry.* By 1939 the "Opry" could be heard on radio nationwide.

Country musicians began to make records in the 1920s. During World War II, many southerners moved to northern cities. Many also served in the military. Country music spread throughout the U.S., Europe, and Asia.

By the 1940s, Nashville was the center for country music. But in the 1950s, many country music fans turned to rock and roll. To win them back, country singers borrowed from pop music. Elvis Presley developed a style called "rockabilly." It mixed country music with rhythm and blues. Later in the 1950s, the "Nashville Sound" appeared. It added elements of pop music to get a bigger audience for country music. By the 1970s, it was hard to tell the difference between the two.

Things changed again in the 1980s. Some musicians felt that country music had become too commercial. Artists such as Johnny Cash, Garth Brooks, and Reba McEntire went back to more traditional country styles. Soon country music was selling more records than ever before.

A First Look at Vocabulary

Choose the best definition for each word in bold type.

_____ 1. If you are looking for the **roots** of country music, go to Nashville.
  a. history   b. performers   c. best parts

_____ 2. A good country music band must have a **fiddle** player.
  a. music   b. banjo   c. violin

_____ 3. Many country music **tunes** have a long history.
  a. songs   b. instruments   c. singers

_____ 4. Today, radio stations **broadcast** country music in nearly every city.
  a. make   b. pay for   c. send out

_____ 5. One famous country music **program** is _Grand Ole Opry_.
  a. style   b. show   c. performer

_____ 6. Two of my friends are country music **fans.**
  a. supporters   b. performers   c. writers

_____ 7. Do you like Willie Nelson's **style** of music?
  a. group of musicians   b. way of playing   c. tunes

_____ 8. The words are one of the important **elements** of country music.
  a. form   b. style   c. part

A Second Look at Vocabulary

Complete the sentences. Use the words from the first exercise.

1. When Willie Nelson came to town, thousands of _____ came to hear him play.

2. The radio station _____ a special music performance.

3. Real fans know the _____ of country music and how it has changed since then.

4. The band has a singer, two guitarists, a drummer, and a _____ player.

5. Country music changed when performers added _____ of different styles of music.

6. Some fans love Elvis Presley's rockabilly _____ of music.

7. Did you see that TV _____ about the Grand Ole Opry last night?

8. "This Face," by Willie Nelson, is one of my favorite country music _____.

72

Understanding the Reading

Choose the best answer.

_____ 1. "Music City, USA," is a nickname for
   a. Chicago, Illinois.
   b. Nashville, Tennessee.
   c. Memphis, Tennessee.

_____ 2. The roots of country music are in
   a. Chicago.
   b. the South.
   c. Europe and Asia.

_____ 3. Elvis Presley's rockabilly style of music mixed country music with
   a. rhythm and blues.
   b. rock and roll.
   c. spirituals.

_____ 4. In the 1980s, country music
   a. added elements of pop music.
   b. lost much of its popularity.
   c. went back to more traditional styles.

_____ 5. At first, *Grand Ole Opry* was called
   a. *WSM Barn Dance.*
   b. *Nashville Sound.*
   c. *National Barn Dance.*

Reading between the Lines

Look carefully at the reading. Mark each statement *T* for *true* or *F* for *false*.

_____ 1. The roots of country music go back to English immigrants who settled in America in the 1700s.

_____ 2. Fiddles were the original instruments used for playing country music.

_____ 3. A Chicago radio station first broadcast *Grand Ole Opry*.

_____ 4. Country music is less popular now than ever before.

_____ 5. Country music spread north during World War II.

What Do You Think?
Discuss these questions.

1. Listen to a country music CD or radio station. Why do many people in the United States like this music? Why do many people in other countries like it?

2. How is country music like rock and roll, blues, or jazz?

3. Love is one of the most common subjects of country music. What else do country singers sing about? Why are these good subjects for country music?

A Last Look
Write about one of these topics.

1. Listen to the music of country music singers from the 1950s and from the 2000s. How is the music alike and different?

2. Read about a country music singer such as Hank Williams, Elvis Presley, Reba McEntire, Patsy Cline, Johnny Cash, or Willie Nelson. Write a short biography.

Eastern Great Lakes Region

Indiana, New York, Ohio, Pennsylvania

A Quick Look at this Region

The five Great Lakes are like inland seas. The Great Lakes feed into the St. Lawrence Seaway. These are among the busiest waterways in North America, transporting millions of tons of products every year.

The French, Dutch, Swedes, and British explored and settled the eastern part of the region in the 16th and 17th centuries. The French were the first to explore and settle lands west of the Appalachians. By the end of the French and Indian Wars in 1754–1763, Britain gained control of the entire area. It became part of the United States after the American Revolution. The region developed rapidly after the Civil War. It became a major center for industry, farming, and finance. Thousands of European immigrants moved here for factory jobs.

The climate of the region is moderate to the south, but winters can be severe in the north. The area east of the lakes often gets heavy snowfall. The region is rich in natural resources. It has good soil, hardwood forests, and valuable minerals such as coal and oil. Today, the region leads the nation in finance and is a leader in manufacturing.

Indiana

Thinking about the Picture

1. What is this car doing? How do you know?
2. Why do people like to race cars?
3. Why do people like to watch car races?

The Indianapolis 500

The Indianapolis 500 is the largest one-day sporting event in the world. Up to 400,000 people attend this famous car race every year. It is held near Indianapolis, Indiana, on the last weekend in May. The oval track is 2.5 miles long and 50 feet wide. The race gets its name because drivers race for 500 miles. They make 200 laps around the track.

The "Indy 500" began early in the 20th century. At the time, Indiana was a center of the new car industry. In 1909, four local businessmen built the Indianapolis Motor Speedway. They wanted a safe place for drivers to test cars at high speeds. They thought sales would improve if they could build faster cars.

The first Indy 500 was held in 1911 at the new Speedway. Until the 1930s, bricks covered the track. Then the owners put asphalt over part of the track. In 1961, they paved the rest. It is now covered with special asphalt, except for the start and finish line. That provides a smooth racing surface. With more than 250,000 permanent seats, the Indianapolis Motor Speedway is the world's largest stadium.

Special companies build Indy cars to reach high speeds. These cars can go from 0 to 100 miles an hour in less than 3 seconds. They are made of carbon fiber. Engineers put wings upside down on the car's nose and tail to press it down on the track. It costs about $2 million a year to maintain an Indy Racing car. Businesses sponsor racing teams as a way to advertise their products. Their car is painted with the company logo. The logo is on the uniforms of drivers and mechanics, too. The first prize is now worth more than $1.5 million.

The fastest Indy qualifying speed record was set in 1996. Arie Luyendyk drove 228.648 miles per hour.

A First Look at Vocabulary

Match each term with its meaning.

_____ 1. lap   a. lasting a long time

_____ 2. asphalt   b. symbol for a company

_____ 3. surface   c. tell about; try to sell

_____ 4. permanent   d. standard clothes worn by a group

_____ 5. stadium   e. the outside or top of something

_____ 6. maintain   f. building where people watch sports

_____ 7. advertise   g. one trip around

_____ 8. logo   h. take care of

_____ 9. uniform   i. black material used for paving roads

A Second Look at Vocabulary

Choose the best answer to complete each sentence.

_____ 1. It takes a very good mechanic to _____ a racing car properly.
     a. advertise   b. drive   c. maintain

_____ 2. Is he the _____ driver, or is this his only race?
     a. famous   b. permanent   c. favorite

_____ 3. A company wants to have a _____ that people will know right away.
     a. logo   b. uniform   c. color

_____ 4. One _____ of the large, oval track was 2.5 miles.
     a. logo   b. lap   c. surface

_____ 5. This city has another _____ where baseball is played.
     a. stadium   b. logo   c. speedway

_____ 6. Everyone who works on the car wears the same _____.
     a. sponsor   b. stadium   c. uniform

_____ 7. The _____ of the road had bumps and holes in it.
     a. surface   b. brick   c. logo

_____ 8. Workmen were putting a fresh layer of _____ on the road.
     a. track   b. asphalt   c. uniform

_____ 9. Companies put logos on cars to _____ their products.
     a. maintain   b. sponsor   c. advertise

Indiana

Understanding the Reading

Choose the best answer.

_____ **1.** How long is the Indianapolis Motor Speedway track?
    a. 500 miles
    b. 2.5 miles
    c. 50 feet

_____ **2.** How long is the Indianapolis 500?
    a. 200 miles
    b. 2.5 miles
    c. 500 miles

_____ **3.** Why did businessmen build the speedway?
    a. They wanted to test cars at high speeds.
    b. They wanted to make money selling tickets.
    c. They wanted to test asphalt as a road surface.

_____ **4.** Why do businesses sponsor racing teams?
    a. They want to improve the safety of the races.
    b. They want to advertise their products.
    c. They can share profits from the races.

_____ **5.** How much does it cost each year to maintain a racing car?
    a. $2 million
    b. $1.5 million
    c. $700,000

Reading between the Lines

Look carefully at the reading. Mark each statement _T_ for _true_ or _F_ for _false_.

_____ **1.** The Indianapolis 500 is held in the spring.

_____ **2.** The race is a bigger event than the World Cup final.

_____ **3.** The track is covered with asphalt because it lasts better than bricks.

_____ **4.** Indy 500 cars travel more than 180 miles an hour.

_____ **5.** Racing cars look just like ordinary cars except they have logos on them.

What Do You Think?
Discuss these questions.

1. Which is more interesting, a car race or a horse race? Why do you think so?

2. Would you like to drive in the Indianapolis 500? Why or why not?

A Last Look
Write about one of these topics.

1. What do car makers and designers learn from auto races? Does racing help improve cars for everyday use?

2. Do research to learn about the risks in car racing. How does it compare to the risks in other sports?

3. What's it like in Indianapolis on the weekend of the Indianapolis 500? Do research and then write a description.

New York

Thinking about the Picture

1. What does the Statue of Liberty make you think about? Why?
2. Why do people enjoy visiting the Statue of Liberty?

The Statue of Liberty and Ellis Island

 Two important U.S. monuments are located on islands in New York Harbor. One is the Statue of Liberty, a tall statue of a woman holding a torch. It is one of the most famous symbols of the United States. The other is the Ellis Island Immigration Museum. "Lady Liberty" stands for freedom, while Ellis Island represents opportunity.

The Statue of Liberty is made of sheets of copper over a steel framework. It is 151 feet, 1 inch tall. Its base is 154 feet high. Liberty holds the flaming torch of freedom in her right hand. On her head, she wears a crown with seven points. They stand for the seven continents and seven seas. At her feet are broken chains. They represent unjust governments that make people suffer. In her left hand is a tablet engraved with the date of the Declaration of Independence—July 4, 1776.

The people of France gave the statue to the people of the United States in 1884. It celebrates the friendship of the two countries and their love of liberty. Americans gave money to build the base.

Tourists come from everywhere to see the Statue of Liberty. Inside the base, they can read a poem by Emma Lazarus. The poem is an invitation to the land of freedom. It begins with these words: "Give me your tired, your poor. . . ." Visitors can climb 192 stairs (or take an elevator) to an observation platform. There are 354 stairs to the top of the crown.

Ellis Island played an important part in the history of U.S. immigration. Beginning in the late 1800s, many people emigrated from eastern and southern Europe. After 1892, they entered the U.S. through Ellis Island. In the next 50 years, about 17 million people passed through. Immigration officials and doctors checked the new arrivals. Two percent were turned away, usually because of illness. The rest began life in the United States. The inspection station closed in 1954. The Ellis Island museum opened in 1990.

A First Look at Vocabulary

Match each term with its meaning.

_____ **1.** statue   a. the act of asking someone to come somewhere

_____ **2.** torches   b. rope made of metal links

_____ **3.** opportunity   c. raised surface to stand on

_____ **4.** crown   d. carved or cut into a surface

_____ **5.** chain   e. burning sticks that give light

_____ **6.** tablet   f. carving or model of a person

_____ **7.** engraved   g. left a country to live in another

_____ **8.** invitation   h. chance to succeed

_____ **9.** platform   i. a piece of wood or stone with words on it

_____ **10.** emigrated   j. head decoration worn to show power

A Second Look at Vocabulary

Complete the sentences. Use the words from the first exercise.

1. People looked for _____ in the U.S. because they wanted to succeed.

2. The speaker stood on a high _____ so everyone could see her.

3. Early people used _____ so they could see at night.

4. When you see the statue, look for the words on the _____.

5. A _____ was wrapped around the prisoner's feet.

6. The _____ said, "Please come to my party."

7. The words were _____ on the hard copper tablet.

8. People _____ to the United States from around the world.

9. An old stone _____ shows us what this person looked like many years ago.

10. The king wore a gold _____ on his head.

Understanding the Reading

Choose the best answer.

_____ **1.** The Statue of Liberty
     a. stands for opportunity for immigrants.
     b. is made of carved stone.
     c. is on an island in New York Harbor.

_____ **2.** The Statue of Liberty shows the friendship of
     a. the people of France and the United States.
     b. the people of different countries and the United States.
     c. rich and poor people in the United States.

_____ **3.** Ellis Island was
     a. the first location of the Statue of Liberty.
     b. the place where 17 million immigrants entered the United States.
     c. given to the United States by France.

Fact or Opinion?

Mark each statement _F_ for _fact_ or _O_ for _opinion_.

_____ **1.** The Statue of Liberty is the most famous symbol of the United States.

_____ **2.** The U.S. put up the Statue of Liberty after people raised money to build a base.

_____ **3.** Many of the people who passed through Ellis Island were from eastern and southern Europe.

_____ **4.** Ellis Island was important in U.S. history.

When Did It Happen?

Write numbers to put the events in the order they happened.

_____ The Ellis Island inspection station was closed.

_____ The Statue of Liberty was given to the United States.

_____ Ellis Island became the gateway to the United States.

_____ The Ellis Island museum was opened.

New York

Ohio

Thinking about the Picture

1. This is an exhibit in the Rock and Roll Hall of Fame. What do you know about rock and roll music? Do you like it?

2. Name some rock musicians. Is their music all the same?

The Rock and Roll Hall of Fame

In 1983, leaders in the music industry decided to honor people who had been important in creating rock and roll. They planned a Rock and Roll Hall of Fame and Museum. They chose Cleveland, Ohio, as its home. The architect I.M. Pei was asked to design it.

People in the music industry chose people for the Hall of Fame. Some were singers and musicians. Others were not performers—they included songwriters, music producers, and disc jockeys. They also honored earlier artists, who came before rock and roll but who influenced it. The first one was Woody Guthrie, a songwriter and folk singer of the 1930s.

Performers can be chosen for the Hall of Fame 25 years after they made their first record. Five to seven new members arc added each year. The Hall of Fame includes many famous names. Some of the first performers chosen were Elvis Presley, Chuck Berry, Bob Dylan, and Aretha Franklin. Early groups included the Beatles, the Beach Boys, the Rolling Stones, and the Supremes. More recent additions are Tina Turner, Elton John, Eric Clapton, Richie Valens, and Bruce Springsteen. Other well-known groups in the Hall include the Grateful Dead, the Bee Gees, and the Mamas and the Papas.

The museum opened in 1995. Exhibits include stage costumes, instruments, and posters. They show how rock and roll has changed. You can see Mick Jagger's stage costumes, Jimi Hendrix's guitar, and John Lennon's "Sergeant Pepper" uniform. Other popular displays are Elvis Presley's black leather outfit, Tina Turner's "Acid Queen" costume, and Madonna's gold stage costume. A new wing opened in 1998.

The Rock and Roll Museum shows how history and politics have influenced popular music—and how popular music has influenced life in the U.S. The museum also does research and gives public programs.

A First Look at Vocabulary

Choose the best definition for each word in bold type.

_____ 1. The **architect** created a special design for the rock and roll museum.
   a. builder   b. manager of band   c. designer of buildings

_____ 2. The **songwriter** played her own song before the audience.
   a. writer of songs   b. guitar player   c. rock and roll star

_____ 3. The radio station hired two new **disc jockeys.**
   a. managers   b. musicians   c. people who play recorded music

_____ 4. Who are your favorite rock and roll **performers?**
   a. styles of music   b. musicians   c. songwriters

_____ 5. People like to see the **costumes** worn by famous musicians.
   a. jewelry   b. instruments   c. stage clothing

_____ 6. The **poster** shows the Rolling Stones playing before an audience.
   a. large picture   b. stage   c. musical instrument

_____ 7. You will want to see the **display** of Madonna's outfits.
   a. costume   b. show   c. announcement

_____ 8. After the museum was open for a few years, a new **wing** was built.
   a. section   b. director   c. museum

A Second Look at Vocabulary

Complete the sentences. Use the words from the first exercise.

1. The _____ in the museum contains pictures, costumes, and musical instruments.

2. A new _____ was built because the museum was too small.

3. The Hall of Fame includes _____, songwriters, and disc jockeys.

4. He wrote several great songs and became a _____ for a rock and roll band.

5. I.M. Pei is a famous _____ who has designed buildings in many countries.

6. The theater hung up a large _____ of the band for that night.

7. Many performers change _____ several times during a performance.

8. If _____ play the recording often enough, people may buy it.

Understanding the Reading

Choose the best answer.

_____ 1. The Rock and Roll Hall of Fame and Museum
   a. is in Cleveland, Ohio.
   b. is open only to people in the music industry.
   c. was the idea of I.M. Pei.

_____ 2. People are chosen for the Hall of Fame by
   a. the owners of the Hall of Fame and Museum.
   b. visitors to the Hall of Fame and Museum.
   c. people in the music industry.

_____ 3. Performers can be chosen for the Hall of Fame
   a. as soon as they sell one million recordings.
   b. 25 years after making their first recording.
   c. when enough fans vote for them.

_____ 4. Each year
   a. about five to seven new members are added to the Hall of Fame.
   b. a new wing is added to the museum.
   c. the museum is moved to a new city.

_____ 5. The museum exhibits
   a. show how history and politics have influenced music.
   b. give visitors the chance to meet and talk with performers.
   c. allow visitors to try on the costumes of famous performers.

Where's the Idea?

These are main ideas from the reading. Write the number of the paragraph where you find each idea.

_____ The museum has exhibits from famous performers.

_____ People in the music industry choose performers and nonperformers to be in the Hall of Fame.

_____ The Rock and Roll Museum shows how music has changed society and been changed by society.

_____ The Rock and Roll Hall of Fame started in 1983.

What Do You Think?
Discuss these questions.

1. Why is rock and roll popular around the world?
2. What makes a rock and roll song popular?
3. What makes a rock and roll performer successful?

A Last Look
Write about one of these topics.

1. Choose a famous rock and roll performer or group. Why did this performer or group become famous? What were the most important songs?
2. Do you like rock and roll? Why or why not? If you prefer another type of music, write about that type.

Ohio

Pennsylvania

Thinking about the Picture

1. Describe this bell. What is wrong with it?
2. Have you heard of the Liberty Bell? What do you think it stands for?

Philadelphia, Birthplace of a Nation

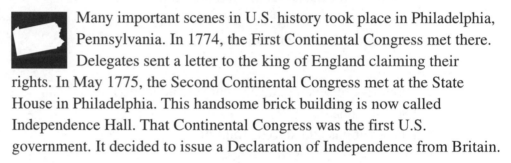 Many important scenes in U.S. history took place in Philadelphia, Pennsylvania. In 1774, the First Continental Congress met there. Delegates sent a letter to the king of England claiming their rights. In May 1775, the Second Continental Congress met at the State House in Philadelphia. This handsome brick building is now called Independence Hall. That Continental Congress was the first U.S. government. It decided to issue a Declaration of Independence from Britain.

On July 4, 1776, delegates approved the document. They voted to make the colonies "free and independent states." Four days later, a crowd waited near the State House. The big bell in the tower rang. People listened while the Declaration of Independence was read aloud. It said that all people had certain rights. These included "life, liberty, and the pursuit of happiness."

The bell in the State House was ordered from England in 1751. Words from the Bible were engraved on it: "Proclaim LIBERTY throughout all the Land unto all the inhabitants thereof" (Leviticus 25:10). When the bell rang the first time, it cracked. After several tries, local workers made a new bell from the metal. It was rung for important events. Today we know it as the Liberty Bell. For safety, the bell was hidden during the Revolution.

In 1787, another convention met in Philadelphia. The new United States needed a better plan of government. Delegates from the 13 states argued for months about details. Finally, the Constitution became the law of the land.

Sometime in the early 1800s, the State House bell cracked again. There are several stories about when and why. It rang for the last time in 1846 to honor Washington's birthday. By then, the bell was a symbol of freedom. After the Civil War, it was sent around the country to reunite Americans. Today the Liberty Bell is kept in a building near Independence Hall. Both are part of Independence National Historical Park.

A First Look at Vocabulary

Choose the best definition for each word in bold type.

_____ 1. The **delegates** could not agree on the wording of the Constitution.

      a. soldiers   b. city leaders   c. representatives

_____ 2. People of the American colonies **claimed** the rights of Englishmen.

      a. said they had   b. gave up   c. asked for

_____ 3. The delegates met in a **handsome** brick building in Philadelphia.

      a. handmade   b. new   c. good-looking

_____ 4. Did anyone **issue** a statement when the bell cracked?

      a. read   b. send out   c. elect

_____ 5. The Declaration of Independence promises the right to the **pursuit** of happiness.

      a. right to   b. hope for   c. search for

_____ 6. The **inhabitants** of the city were happy to hear the bell ring.

      a. visitors   b. people living there   c. delegates

_____ 7. During which **convention** did delegates approve the Constitution?

      a. meeting   b. government   c. war

_____ 8. After the Civil War, Americans had to **reunite.**

      a. come together again   b. forgive each other   c. go to war

A Second Look at Vocabulary

Complete the sentences. Use the words from the first exercise.

1. Philadelphia is a _____ city with many beautiful buildings.

2. The U.S. held a _____ in Philadelphia in 1787.

3. After a war divides a country, people need to _____.

4. Which delegates agreed to _____ the Declaration of Independence?

5. How many _____ were chosen to represent each colony?

6. The _____ of Philadelphia are proud of their city's history.

7. Is the _____ of freedom more important than the search for happiness?

8. The delegates _____ their rights from the king.

Understanding the Reading

Choose the best answer.

_____ 1. The Second Continental Congress
   a. issued the Declaration of Independence.
   b. met in New York City.
   c. ordered the bell, which later was called the Liberty Bell.

_____ 2. Which of these quotes is from the Declaration of Independence?
   a. "Proclaim liberty throughout all the land unto all the inhabitants."
   b. "We the people of the United States . . . do ordain and establish this Constitution."
   c. "life, liberty, and the pursuit of happiness."

_____ 3. When the Declaration of Independence was first read to the people in Philadelphia in 1776, the Liberty Bell
   a. cracked for the second time.
   b. was rung.
   c. was hidden to keep it safe.

When Did It Happen?

Write numbers to put the events in the order they happened.

_____ The Declaration of Independence was approved.

_____ The U.S. Constitution was written.

_____ The First Continental Congress met in Philadelphia.

Reading between the Lines

Look carefully at the reading. Mark each statement _T_ for _true_ or _F_ for _false_.

_____ 1. The first U.S. government met in Philadelphia.

_____ 2. The Constitution is the only plan of government the U.S. has ever had.

_____ 3. The Liberty Bell has not been rung in more than 150 years.

_____ 4. The Liberty Bell is in the bell tower on Independence Hall.

What Do You Think?

Discuss these questions.

1. The Liberty Bell is a national symbol of freedom. Why do people need national symbols like this one? What other national symbols can you name?

2. Philadelphia is called "the Birthplace of a Nation." Do you think this is a good nickname for Philadelphia? Explain your answer.

A Last Look

Write about one of these topics.

1. The Declaration of Independence is considered one of the world's most important documents. Why do you think this is true?

2. The people of many nations have revolted, or broken away from, their governments. Find out about one revolution. Why did the people revolt against their rulers?

Western Great Lakes Region

Illinois, Iowa, Michigan, Minnesota, Missouri, Wisconsin

A Quick Look at this Region

Most of the western Great Lakes region was first explored and settled by the French. Lands east of the Mississippi River were given to Great Britain after the French and Indian Wars of 1754–1763. France sold lands west of the Mississippi to the United States in 1803 as the Louisiana Purchase.

This region has the longest and most important rivers and lakes in North America. It borders the western portions of the Great Lakes. It is divided down the middle by the Mississippi River. The Missouri and Ohio Rivers enter the Mississippi from the west and east. Winters can be very cold in the northern parts of the region. The weather moderates quickly toward the south.

The first European settlers came to the region to trade with Native Americans. Later they came to mine for lead and iron ore. Others came to farm the rich land and to cut timber from the vast forests of the north. Today, manufacturing and transportation provide many of the economic opportunities. The region is a leader in making cars and aircraft. Corn, soybeans, and dairy cattle are important in farming.

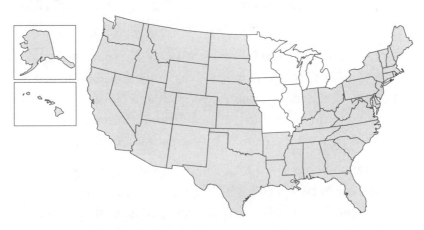

Illinois

Thinking about the Picture
1. Who was Abraham Lincoln?
2. What major event happened while Lincoln was president?
3. Why do people remember him today?

Abraham Lincoln

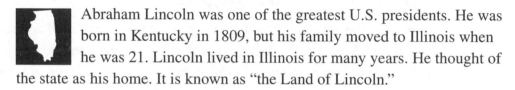

Abraham Lincoln was one of the greatest U.S. presidents. He was born in Kentucky in 1809, but his family moved to Illinois when he was 21. Lincoln lived in Illinois for many years. He thought of the state as his home. It is known as "the Land of Lincoln."

Lincoln's family was poor. He grew up in a log cabin, then worked as a store clerk and on a riverboat. Lincoln studied to be a lawyer by reading law books. In 1837, he opened a law office in Springfield, Illinois. He was elected to Congress in 1846. Two years later, he returned to Springfield.

The question of slavery was crucial in U.S. politics. Lincoln became leader of the new Republican Party in Illinois. The party opposed slavery. In 1858, he ran against Stephen A. Douglas for the U.S. Senate. In debates during the campaign, Lincoln argued that slavery should not be allowed in new states. He lost the election, but the debates made him famous.

In 1860, Lincoln was the Republican candidate for president—and won. In response, most southern states seceded from the United States. They formed a new government, the Confederacy. By April 1861, the Civil War was underway. Lincoln wanted to keep the nation whole.

On January 1, 1863, President Lincoln issued the Emancipation Proclamation. It said that all slaves in the Confederate states were free. Lincoln made many famous speeches. On November 19, 1863, he spoke at a cemetery in Gettysburg, Pennsylvania. He spoke about the importance of "government of the people, by the people, for the people."

Many people loved Lincoln, but many others hated him. The Civil War ended on April 9, 1865. Five days later, John Wilkes Booth assassinated the president. Thousands of people watched as Lincoln's funeral train crossed the country. It took him home to Springfield, Illinois.

A First Look at Vocabulary

Match each term with its meaning.

_____ **1.** clerk

_____ **2.** lawyer

_____ **3.** crucial

_____ **4.** politics

_____ **5.** opposed

_____ **6.** debate

_____ **7.** campaign

_____ **8.** cemetery

_____ **9.** assassinated

a. effort to get elected

b. murdered

c. place where the dead are buried; graveyard

d. person who knows about the law

e. someone who sells things in a store

f. very important

g. was against

h. formal argument

i. way of governing; ideas about governing

A Second Look at Vocabulary

Choose the best answer to complete each sentence.

_____ **1.** In _____, a person's goal is to be elected to a government office.
    a. education   b. war   c. politics

_____ **2.** Do you think Stephen Douglas _____ or supported slavery?
    a. opposed   b. debated   c. seceded

_____ **3.** Booth _____ President Lincoln with a gun.
    a. fought   b. debated   c. assassinated

_____ **4.** When Lincoln was a _____, what kind of products did he sell?
    a. politician   b. clerk   c. president

_____ **5.** The _____ issue of Lincoln's time was slavery. It had to be ended.
    a. crucial   b. forgotten   c. least memorable

_____ **6.** Someone who breaks the law may want a _____.
    a. clerk   b. politician   c. lawyer

_____ **7.** Lincoln and Douglas argued their view during their _____.
    a. politics   b. debates   c. election

_____ **8.** During the _____, Lincoln told people why he should be elected.
    a. voting   b. campaign   c. politics

_____ **9.** Men who had died in battle were buried in the _____.
    a. campaign   b. field   c. cemetery

Understanding the Reading

Choose the best answer.

_____ 1. Abraham Lincoln was born in Kentucky
    a. but moved to Illinois when he was 21.
    b. and lived there most of his life.
    c. but moved to Illinois after he was elected president.

_____ 2. Lincoln's famous debates with Stephen Douglas happened when he ran for
    a. president.
    b. Congress.
    c. the U.S. Senate.

_____ 3. When the Civil War began, Lincoln wanted
    a. to keep all the states in the Union.
    b. to force the slave states to leave the Union.
    c. to keep peace between the states.

_____ 4. The Emancipation Proclamation
    a. honored the soldiers who died in the Civil War.
    b. freed slaves in the Confederate states.
    c. ended the Civil War.

_____ 5. Lincoln was assassinated
    a. shortly before the Civil War ended.
    b. shortly after he was elected president.
    c. shortly after the Civil War ended.

Fact or Opinion?

Mark each statement *F* for *fact* or *O* for *opinion*.

_____ 1. Abraham Lincoln was America's greatest president.

_____ 2. Because Lincoln was elected president, most Southern states seceded from the Union.

_____ 3. Lincoln believed in "government of the people, by the people, for the people."

_____ 4. Abraham Lincoln won his debates with Stephen Douglas.

_____ 5. The Confederate states were wrong in seceding from the United States.

What Do You Think?
Discuss these questions.

1. Would Lincoln be remembered as a great president if the Civil War had not happened?

2. How should Americans honor the memory of Abraham Lincoln?

A Last Look
Write about one of these topics.

1. Read about the assassination of Lincoln, his funeral, and how the people responded to the news of his death. Write a summary of what you have learned.

2. Lincoln's Gettysburg Address is one of the greatest speeches by a U.S. president. Read the speech. Tell what you think of it.

Iowa

Thinking about the Picture

1. What are these animals? Why would they be shown at a fair?
2. Have you been to a state or agricultural fair? Describe it. Did you enjoy it?

State Fair

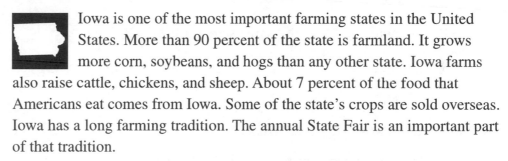

Iowa is one of the most important farming states in the United States. More than 90 percent of the state is farmland. It grows more corn, soybeans, and hogs than any other state. Iowa farms also raise cattle, chickens, and sheep. About 7 percent of the food that Americans eat comes from Iowa. Some of the state's crops are sold overseas. Iowa has a long farming tradition. The annual State Fair is an important part of that tradition.

Many states, especially farming states, hold state fairs. They are a way to celebrate the harvest. The Iowa State Fair is one of the oldest and largest. The fair was first held in 1854. In the early days, it took place in different parts of the state. Since 1878, it has been held each year in Des Moines, the capital. It is one of the state's most important events.

More than 900,000 people visit the Iowa State Fair every year. It lasts for 11 days in August. The fair is a showcase for farming, industry, and entertainment. Visitors can enjoy Ferris wheels and other rides. They can play games and watch demonstrations. Large exhibit buildings display farm equipment and other products. Farm families bring their best animals to compete for prizes. Hundreds of displays show off fruits, vegetables, and handicrafts. People also look forward to unusual attractions. One State Fair tradition is butter sculpture. An artist might shape a life-size cow out of more than 500 pounds of butter.

Crowds of fairgoers enjoy free entertainment, too. Well-known performers such as Chuck Berry, Johnny Cash, Sonny and Cher, and Garth Brooks have performed there. In 1975, more than 25,000 people saw a single performance by the Beach Boys. Many recent U.S. presidents have also visited the Iowa State Fair.

A First Look at Vocabulary

Match each term with its meaning.

_____ **1.** overseas   a. try to win

_____ **2.** fair   b. showing how something works

_____ **3.** celebrate   c. across the ocean; in other countries

_____ **4.** harvest   d. a show for farm, household, or other products

_____ **5.** lasts   e. do something to enjoy a special event

_____ **6.** demonstration   f. products made by hand

_____ **7.** life-size   g. continues

_____ **8.** compete   h. same size as the actual thing

_____ **9.** handicrafts   i. gathering of crops after the growing season

A Second Look at Vocabulary

Complete the sentences. Use the words in the box.

celebrate	demonstration	handicrafts	lasts	overseas
compete	fair	harvest	life-size	

1. The _____ butter sculpture shows how big a real cow is.

2. Quilts, baskets, and other _____ are shown in another display.

3. When farmers have good crops, they should _____.

4. Boys and girls _____ for prizes for growing the best pigs.

5. Corn is sold _____ to countries like Russia and China.

6. There is a _____ on how to use the newest farm equipment.

7. In some places, the harvest _____ from August through November.

8. Farmers work hard during _____ to bring in their crops.

9. You can see farm animals and crops on display at the _____.

Understanding the Reading

Choose the best answer.

_____ 1. Iowa is one of the most important
   a. business states in the United States.
   b. industrial states in the United States.
   c. farming states in the United States.

_____ 2. The Iowa State Fair is
   a. one of the oldest and largest fairs in the United States.
   b. the only state fair in the United States.
   c. the only state fair that celebrates the harvest.

_____ 3. The Iowa State Fair is
   a. seen by more than 2 million people each year.
   b. held in Des Moines each year.
   c. held in a different city in Iowa each year.

Reading between the Lines

Look carefully at the reading. Mark each statement _T_ for _true_ or _F_ for _false_.

_____ 1. Less than 10 percent of the land in Iowa is not used for farming.

_____ 2. Iowa sends most of its farm products to other countries.

_____ 3. Few people know about the State Fair outside of Iowa.

_____ 4. The Iowa State Fair has entertainment for everyone in the family.

Fact or Opinion?

Mark each statement _F_ for _fact_ or _O_ for _opinion_.

_____ 1. Large numbers of people attend the Iowa State Fair.

_____ 2. The Iowa State Fair is an interesting place to visit.

_____ 3. The State Fair has a large variety of exhibits and activities.

_____ 4. The State Fair has the best musical performers in the state.

What Do You Think?
Discuss these questions.

1. Many people who live in cities and towns go to state fairs. Why do these people go to state fairs?

2. Why do presidents attend the Iowa State Fair?

A Last Look
Write about one of these topics.

1. What kinds of contests are held for crops and animals at the Iowa State Fair? Why are there separate contests for children and adults? Why do you think the fair has these contests?

2. Why do Iowa and other states have state fairs? Is it just to showcase farming? Are there other reasons?

Iowa

Michigan

Thinking about the Picture
1. What is being made in this picture?
2. When was this picture taken? How do you know?
3. How have cars changed since this picture was taken?

The Automobile Industry

 One nickname for the city of Detroit is "Motor City." Another is "Automobile Capital of the World." Those names show how important the automobile industry is to Michigan.

Michigan has a long history as a center of the auto industry. Two pioneers of the industry worked there. In 1896, Henry Ford built a passenger car in Dearborn, Michigan. He started the Ford Motor Company. The same year, Ransom Eli Olds made a car in Lansing, Michigan. In 1899, he helped start the Oldsmobile Automobile Company in Detroit.

The auto industry invented new ways of production. Early automobiles were made by hand one at a time. In 1901, the Oldsmobile Company started using "mass production." It made identical car parts all at one time. Then cars were put together using these parts. Cars made this way were much cheaper. In 1908, Henry Ford introduced the moving "assembly line." It turned out the popular "Model T." Cars were moved along on a conveyor belt from worker to worker. Each worker did one job. One added a fender. Another tightened a bolt. Cars could be built cheaper and faster than before. Working people could afford to buy a car. By the 1920s Michigan was the leading producer of cars, trucks, and vans.

In the 1970s, the U.S. auto industry faced problems. Gasoline became very expensive. Cars made in Detroit were large and used a lot of gas. Car makers in Europe and Japan were making smaller cars that used less gas. To compete, Michigan car makers also built small cars.

Then in 1984, car makers introduced very large, boxy passenger cars. They were called "minivans" or "sports utility vehicles" (SUVs). Although they used a lot of gas, they became very popular. By the 1990s, SUVs were very common on American highways.

Michigan

A First Look at Vocabulary

Choose the best definition for each word in bold type.

_____ **1.** About 4.5 million people live in **metropolitan** Detroit.

    a. modern   b. area near a city   c. oldest part of

_____ **2.** Henry Ford was one of the **pioneers** in car making.

    a. people who led the way   b. people who followed   c. owners

_____ **3.** Most **passenger** cars have room for at least four people.

    a. especially large   b. to carry products   c. to carry people

_____ **4.** Car makers want to improve their ways of **production.**

    a. designing things   b. making things   c. selling things

_____ **5.** Cars are made with **identical** parts.

    a. different   b. nearly the same   c. exactly the same

_____ **6.** The assembly line made it possible to sell **cheaper** cars.

    a. less costly   b. more convenient   c. faster

_____ **7.** Today, more people can **afford** new cars.

    a. be able to pay for   b. be able to drive   c. want to have

_____ **8.** Many people buy **foreign** cars.

    a. American   b. from other countries   c. locally made

A Second Look at Vocabulary

Complete the sentences. Use the words from the first exercise.

1. Well-trained workers are needed for the _____ of automobiles.

2. You might buy a used car if you cannot _____ a new one.

3. _____ Detroit includes the city and the towns around it.

4. A _____ car will often last as long as a more costly one.

5. Two cars may use _____ parts inside but look very different.

6. Both U.S.-made cars and _____ cars are popular in the United States.

7. _____ in any industry must have imagination and be willing to take risks.

Understanding the Reading

Choose the best answer.

_____ **1.** Detroit is sometimes called the
    a. "Industrial Capital of North America."
    b. "Automobile Capital of the World."
    c. "Home of Henry Ford and Ransom Olds."

_____ **2.** Two pioneers of the automobile industry were
    a. Henry Ford and Thomas Edison.
    b. Ransom Eli Olds and Thomas Edison.
    c. Ransom Eli Olds and Henry Ford.

_____ **3.** The Oldsmobile Company was the first car company to use
    a. the assembly line.
    b. the conveyor belt.
    c. mass production.

_____ **4.** In the 1970s, the U.S. car industry had problems because
    a. gas became very expensive.
    b. workers wanted more money.
    c. cars became too expensive.

_____ **5.** In the 1990s, one of the most common cars was the
    a. Model T.
    b. SUV.
    c. Oldsmobile.

When Did It Happen?

Write numbers to put the events in the order they happened.

_____ Ransom Eli Olds started a car company in Detroit.

_____ Car makers introduced minivans.

_____ Henry Ford built a passenger car in Dearborn, Michigan.

_____ Michigan became the biggest maker of cars, trucks, and vans.

_____ Car makers began using mass production to make cars.

_____ Henry Ford began making cars on an assembly line.

What Do You Think?

Discuss these questions.

1. Many people in the U.S. buy foreign cars. Is that right or wrong? Why?
2. Why are minivans and SUVs so popular today?
3. What things are most important when someone chooses a car?

A Last Look

Write about one of these topics.

1. Learn about the kinds of cars that people will be driving in the future. Do you want one of these new cars? Why or why not?
2. What suggestions do you have for reducing the number of car accidents?

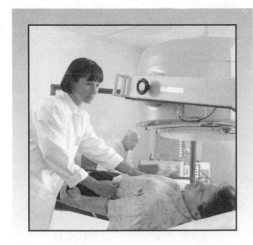

Minnesota

Thinking about the Picture

1. What is happening in this picture?
2. Who do you see when you are sick or hurt?
3. What are some ways in which doctors help people?

Mayo Clinic

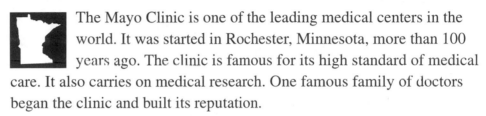 The Mayo Clinic is one of the leading medical centers in the world. It was started in Rochester, Minnesota, more than 100 years ago. The clinic is famous for its high standard of medical care. It also carries on medical research. One famous family of doctors began the clinic and built its reputation.

William Worrall Mayo came to the United States from England in 1845. He studied medicine and then moved to Minnesota. In 1863 he opened an office in Rochester, Minnesota. His son William James Mayo was born in 1861. Another son, Charles Horace Mayo, was born in 1865. When the two boys grew up, they went to medical school. Both joined their father's medical practice. Later, Charles's son also became a doctor and joined the family clinic. All the Mayos were skillful surgeons.

In 1892, the Mayos began to invite other doctors to join their clinic. Each doctor had a specialty, but all worked together. It was one of the first "group practices" in medicine. Doctors around the world began to copy this model. Each doctor in a clinic has a specialty. One doctor studies a patient's problems. Then he or she can ask the clinic's specialists for advice.

Over the years, the Mayo Clinic has been the first in many ways. In 1915 it set up a foundation for medical education and research. It began a program to train doctors as specialists. Mayo Clinic doctors were the first to use cortisone for one type of arthritis. They invented instruments for open-heart surgery. They also set up the nation's first blood bank.

Today, the Mayo Clinic staff includes nearly 900 doctors and medical scientists. Its medical school trains physicians in more than 100 specialties. It has opened clinics in other states, such as Florida and Arizona. Patients from all over the world travel to the clinic because of its fine reputation.

A First Look at Vocabulary

Choose the best definition for each word in bold type.

_____ 1. Every community should have a health **clinic.**
   a. library   b. medical school   c. medical office

_____ 2. Scientists do **research** to learn about diseases.
   a. treatment   b. studies   c. surgery

_____ 3. A **surgeon** must know how each body part works.
   a. medical student   b. doctor who cuts out diseased parts   c. doctor who prescribes drugs

_____ 4. If you have certain types of illness, find a doctor with that **specialty.**
   a. popularity   b. field of study   c. clinic

_____ 5. Several doctors work together in a **group practice.**
   a. medical center   b. learning center   c. office of several doctors

_____ 6. Doctors try to help **patients** recover from disease.
   a. quiet people   b. nurses   c. people they treat

_____ 7. Special **instruments** are used for heart surgery.
   a. tools   b. doctors   c. offices

_____ 8. **Physicians** go to medical school for many years.
   a. teachers   b. doctors   c. nurses

A Second Look at Vocabulary

Complete the sentences. Use the words from the first exercise.

1. Different _____ need different kinds of care.

2. When William Worrall Mayo and his sons joined with other doctors, they formed

   a _____.

3. A _____ needs skillful, steady hands.

4. A physician with a _____ is called a specialist.

5. _____ need a medical license before they can treat patients.

6. The best _____ for surgery are costly.

7. A _____ could have many doctors or just one.

Understanding the Reading

Choose the best answer.

_____ **1.** The Mayo Clinic was started in
   a. Minneapolis.
   b. Rochester.
   c. Florida.

_____ **2.** The Mayo Clinic was the first in the United States to
   a. set up a blood bank.
   b. do open-heart surgery.
   c. train doctors as specialists.

_____ **3.** The Mayo Clinic
   a. provides medical care only for the people of Minnesota.
   b. still operates as a group practice with just a few doctors.
   c. has opened clinics in Florida and Arizona.

Fact or Opinion?

Mark each statement _F_ for _fact_ or _O_ for _opinion_.

_____ **1.** The Mayo Clinic is the world's leading medical center.

_____ **2.** People come to the Mayo Clinic because of its reputation.

_____ **3.** Patients get better care because doctors from different specialties work together in helping them.

_____ **4.** Doctors in other countries thought the Mayos' plan for group practices was a good idea.

When Did It Happen?

Write numbers to put the events in the order they happened.

_____ William Mayo started a medical practice in Minnesota.

_____ The Mayos asked other doctors to join their clinic.

_____ The clinic set up a foundation for research and education.

_____ William Worrall Mayo's sons joined his medical practice.

What Do You Think?
Discuss these questions.

1. Why do people travel long distances to places like the Mayo Clinic? Is it worth it?

2. If you or someone in your family had a serious disease, would you go to the Mayo Clinic? Why or why not?

3. Many people think medical care costs too much. Can anything be done to make it less expensive?

A Last Look
Write about one of these topics.

1. What kind of education is needed to become a doctor? How long does it take?

2. What do you think is the most serious disease today? Why is it important to find a cure?

3. What are some medical centers in your region? Where are they? What is their reputation for health care?

Hulton Archive/Getty Images

Missouri

Thinking about the Picture

1. Describe Mark Twain. What words would you use to describe his hair, mustache, and eyebrows?

2. What can you tell about his personality?

Mark Twain

Mark Twain is one of the greatest U.S. writers. He is known for his special style of humor and his pictures of American life. In the late 1800s, people throughout the United States and Europe immediately recognized the man in the white suit with the white hair and bushy mustache. Even when he was world-famous, Twain's roots were in Missouri. Many of his best stories were about his boyhood there.

Twain's real name was Samuel Langhorne Clemens. "Mark Twain" was a pen name. It came from the language used by crews on riverboats. The words "mark twain" told how deep the water in the river was.

Sam Clemens was born in Florida, Missouri, in 1835. The evening he was born, Halley's Comet shone in the sky. According to one story, his mother said it meant her son would be rich and famous. The family later moved to Hannibal, Missouri, a town on the Mississippi River. Young Sam's first ambition was to be a pilot for riverboats.

When he grew up, Clemens took many different jobs. He worked as a steamboat pilot. Then he wrote travel letters and articles. In 1861 he became a reporter for a Nevada newspaper. In 1865, he wrote a story about a "Celebrated Jumping Frog." That story made him famous.

Twain went on to write many popular books. He published *The Adventures of Tom Sawyer* in 1876. It was based on his childhood in Hannibal. He wrote about his travels in Europe and the United States. In 1884, Mark Twain published what many think was his greatest book, *Huckleberry Finn*. It gave a picture of life in the South before the Civil War.

When Mark Twain died in 1910, Halley's Comet was again in the sky. People everywhere mourned his death. Twain was the voice of the spirit of the real America.

A First Look at Vocabulary

Choose the best definition for each word in bold type.

_____ 1. Mark Twain used **humor** even about serious topics.
    a. stories   b. anger   c. something funny

_____ 2. Mark Twain's **mustache** grew long and bushy.
    a. hair on lip   b. hair above eyes   c. hair on head

_____ 3. "Mark Twain" was the **pen name** of Samuel Clemens.
    a. real name   b. writer's name   c. first name

_____ 4. After he reached his first **ambition,** Clemens began to travel.
    a. town   b. job   c. goal

_____ 5. The pilot of a **steamboat** knew every bend in the river.
    a. boat powered by steam   b. electric boat   c. boat for canals

_____ 6. A good **reporter** tells only the facts.
    a. novelist   b. poet   c. news writer

_____ 7. *Huckleberry Finn* was **published** in 1884.
    a. made famous   b. brought out for sale   c. written

_____ 8. People **mourned** the death of this great writer.
    a. were saddened by   b. wrote about   c. were interested in

A Second Look at Vocabulary

Complete the sentences. Use the words from the first exercise.

1. Samuel Clemens _____ the death of his daughter, Jean, in 1909.

2. Many people do not know that "Mark Twain" is the _____ of Samuel Clemens.

3. Mark Twain became famous for his _____ because he wrote funny stories.

4. As a _____, Twain wrote news stories about life in Nevada.

5. Did Twain have the _____ to become a riverboat pilot?

6. Of all the books _____ by Mark Twain, *Huckleberry Finn* is the most famous.

7. Twain's long, bushy _____ covered both his upper and lower lips.

8. Twain enjoyed his years working on the river as a _____ pilot.

Missouri

Understanding the Reading

Choose the best answer.

_____ **1.** Many of Mark Twain's best stories
  a. told about life in Nevada.
  b. told about life in Missouri.
  c. told about his life on riverboats.

_____ **2.** Samuel Clemens's pen name, "Mark Twain,"
  a. describes how deep the river was.
  b. comes from words used in newspaper writing.
  c. is the name of a comet that appeared when he was born.

_____ **3.** Samuel Clemens grew up in
  a. St. Louis.
  b. Hannibal.
  c. Florida.

_____ **4.** Mark Twain had many jobs, including
  a. newspaper reporter, politician, and steamboat pilot.
  b. steamboat pilot, soldier, and scientist.
  c. steamboat pilot, newspaper reporter, and novelist.

Fact or Opinion?

Mark each statement _F_ for _fact_ or _O_ for _opinion_.

_____ **1.** Halley's Comet was shining when Twain was born and when he died.

_____ **2.** Mark Twain grew up near the Mississippi River.

_____ **3.** No other writer used humor as well as Mark Twain.

When Did It Happen?

Write numbers to put the events in the order they happened.

_____ Mark Twain wrote "The Celebrated Jumping Frog."

_____ Mark Twain's family moved to Hannibal.

_____ Mark Twain published _Huckleberry Finn._

_____ Mark Twain worked as a steamboat pilot.

What Do You Think?
Discuss these questions.

1. Look at a map of the United States. Why was the Mississippi River important in the 1800s?

2. Mark Twain was famous for his humor. Why is humor useful when discussing serious subjects?

A Last Look
Write about one of these topics.

1. Read some quotes by Mark Twain. Which are your favorites? Why?

2. The town of Hannibal is proud to be the birthplace of Mark Twain. Describe some of the buildings and other places you would see if you visited there.

3. Read more about Twain and the books and stories he wrote. What are some things he wrote about?

Wisconsin

Thinking about the Picture

1. What is this woman riding?
2. What can you tell about the woman from her expression?
3. Why do people enjoy riding motorcycles?

Harley-Davidson

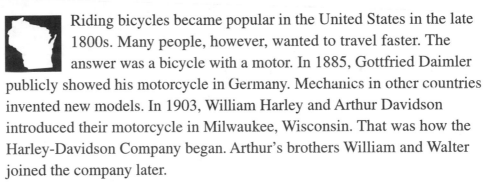

Riding bicycles became popular in the United States in the late 1800s. Many people, however, wanted to travel faster. The answer was a bicycle with a motor. In 1885, Gottfried Daimler publicly showed his motorcycle in Germany. Mechanics in other countries invented new models. In 1903, William Harley and Arthur Davidson introduced their motorcycle in Milwaukee, Wisconsin. That was how the Harley-Davidson Company began. Arthur's brothers William and Walter joined the company later.

In 1909, the company improved its engine. The new design had two cylinders that formed a "V-twin." Since then, other improvements have been made, but the same kind of engine is still used today.

Harley-Davidson began to sell motorcycles to the police and the military. During World War I, the U.S. Army bought 20,000 motorcycles, most of them Harleys. In World War II, the company sold more than 90,000 motorcycles for military use.

In the 1940s, Harley-Davidson began to sell black boots and leather jackets to its bikers. Soon this clothing was the uniform of "motorcycle culture." Bikes and leather jackets became symbols of rebellion against an older generation. Once there were 150 motorcycle companies in the United States. In 1953, Harley-Davidson became the only one.

In the 1970s, many bikers turned to Japanese motorcycles. They were less expensive. Harley-Davidson's share of the market dropped sharply. In 1983 the U.S. government placed a tax on imported heavyweight motorcycles. In 1987, the company asked that the tax be lifted.

Today Harleys are sold all around the world. The average owner is a man in his mid-40s, with a high income. He often rides with other bikers for fun.

A First Look at Vocabulary

Match each term with its meaning.

_____ **1.** publicly   a. brought into a country

_____ **2.** mechanic   b. all the people of about the same age

_____ **3.** military   c. typical

_____ **4.** generation   d. in front of everyone

_____ **5.** quality   e. part

_____ **6.** share   f. armed forces

_____ **7.** imported   g. level of excellence

_____ **8.** average   h. someone who works on engines

A Second Look at Vocabulary

Choose the best answer to complete each sentence.

_____ **1.** A large crowd came to listen when the new motorcycle was ____ introduced.
     a. quietly   b. publicly   c. privately

_____ **2.** A good ____ can keep older Harley-Davidsons running well.
     a. uniform   b. biker   c. mechanic

_____ **3.** The ____ used motorcycles to deliver messages during wartime.
     a. military   b. public   c. company

_____ **4.** Now the older ____ rides Harleys as well as younger people.
     a. engine   b. military   c. generation

_____ **5.** Because Harley-Davidsons are carefully built, they are known for
their high ____.
     a. symbol   b. quality   c. uniform

_____ **6.** A big ____ of older motorcycle riders buy Harleys.
     a. share   b. quality   c. generation

_____ **7.** Many people buy Japanese motorcycles, which are ____ from Asia.
     a. shared   b. imported   c. taxed

_____ **8.** The ____ Harley owner rides for pleasure.
     a. public   b. improved   c. average

Wisconsin

Understanding the Reading

Choose the best answer.

_____ **1.** In 1903, William Harley and Arthur Davidson began building motorcycles
   a. in Milwaukee.
   b. in Japan.
   c. for the U.S. government.

_____ **2.** In 1909, Harley-Davidson introduced
   a. a motorcycle made for the military.
   b. the first motorcycle made in America.
   c. the V-twin engine that is still made today.

_____ **3.** Black boots and leather jackets became popular
   a. at the beginning of the 20th century.
   b. in the 1940s.
   c. in the 1970s.

Reading between the Lines

Look carefully at the reading. Mark each statement _T_ for _true_ or _F_ for _false_.

_____ **1.** Harley-Davidson has built the same kind of engine since 1909.

_____ **2.** Today, Harley-Davidson is one of about 150 motorcycle companies in the United States.

_____ **3.** Most bikers buy Harleys because they are not expensive.

_____ **4.** In the 1940s, people bought Harleys as an act of rebellion.

When Did It Happen?

Write numbers to put the events in the order they happened.

_____ The U.S. government began taxing imported motorcycles.

_____ The Harley-Davidson company designed a V-twin engine.

_____ The company began selling black boots and leather jackets.

_____ Harley-Davidson became the last American motorcycle company.

What Do You Think?

Discuss these questions.

1. Why are many Harley-Davidson bikers middle-aged?
2. Why do police use motorcycles? Why are they sometimes better than cars?
3. Why do you think the government began taxing imported motorcycles in 1983? Why would Harley-Davidson ask the government to lift this tax in 1987?

A Last Look

Write about one of these topics.

1. Would you like to own a Harley-Davidson? Why or why not?
2. Do you think Harley-Davidsons are still a symbol of rebellion? Explain.

Great Plains/Rocky Mountain Region

Colorado, Idaho, Kansas, Montana, Nebraska, Nevada, North Dakota, South Dakota, Utah, Wyoming

A Quick Look at the Region

The region was first explored by the Spanish in the 1500s. Later, the land became part of the United States. Lewis and Clark led their famous expedition across the northern parts of the region. However, the region developed slowly. Settlers passed through, but didn't stop and build homes.

The land seemed harsh and dangerous. The Great Plains are dry grassland. The winters are cold and the summers are hot with little rain. The Rocky Mountains have steep mountains, large deserts, and high plateaus. Winters are cold, and some places have deep snow.

The Homestead Act of 1862 encouraged farmers to move west. Many settled on the Great Plains. Ranchers came to raise cattle. Railroads crossed the plains, bringing more jobs and families. In the 1850s and 1870s, gold, silver, and other metals were discovered in the Rocky Mountains. People flocked to the region.

Mining, farming, and cattle raising are still major industries. Tourism is also important to the economy. People go to the mountains for the scenery and winter sports. Gambling is important in Nevada.

Colorado

Thinking about the Picture

1. What is this man doing? What equipment does he use?
2. Why do people like to ski?
3. Where do people go to ski?

Winter Sports

 Ninety-one mountains in the United States are over 14,000 feet tall. About 55 of them are in Colorado. The mountains are one reason that millions of tourists visit the state every year.

Skiing has been popular in parts of Europe for hundreds of years. But there, it was not just a sport. It was a practical way to travel in snowy weather. Norwegian immigrants brought skiing to the United States in the 1800s, but it did not become popular here until many years later.

In the U.S., skiing and ski jumping began in the town of Steamboat Springs, Colorado. A Norwegian skier, Carl Howelson, introduced them in 1912. The sport began to become popular after World War I. Rich Americans were able to travel to Europe. Many enjoyed skiing on their trips. By the 1930s, Steamboat Springs was widely known as a ski center. In 1936, Aspen, Colorado, also built a ski center. Aspen held its first downhill races in 1937. After World War II, more ski resorts opened in Colorado.

Skiers in the 1930s and 1940s looked very different from today. There were no special ski clothes. Men sometimes skied in coats and ties. Often they wore business shirts under plain sweaters. Now skiers wear colorful clothing, ski pants, and parkas. They wear special goggles to protect their eyes from the sun and the glare on the snow.

The sport has changed in other ways, too. At first, skis were made of wood. They were heavy and hard to turn. Lighter aluminum or fiberglass skis made skiing much easier. Ski lifts were another invention. Skiers could ride the lift up the mountain, then ski down.

Today, Colorado has more than 40 ski resorts. Aspen, Boulder, and Vail are some of the most famous. International ski races take place each year in Colorado. The world's best skiers go there to compete.

A First Look at Vocabulary

Choose the best definition for each word in bold type.

_____ 1. The **tourists** enjoyed the mountains and went skiing every day.
   a. people who travel for fun   b. people who work   c. people who ski

_____ 2. The tourist said the mountain **scenery** was wonderful.
   a. people   b. outdoor surroundings   c. weather

_____ 3. Many people stood at the bottom of the hill to see who won the **downhill** race.
   a. skiing across a field   b. skiing down a hill   c. riding a ski lift

_____ 4. It was very cold, so everyone wore **parkas.**
   a. heavy gloves   b. heavy sweaters   c. heavy coats

_____ 5. The skiers wore **goggles** for protection from the sun.
   a. special eyeglasses   b. heavy gloves   c. heavy coats

_____ 6. The **glare** of the sun on the snow was very bright.
   a. rising   b. setting   c. bright shine

_____ 7. The **fiberglass** skis are much lighter than the old wooden ones.
   a. plastic   b. spun glass   c. wooden

_____ 8. The town held a snow **festival** every January.
   a. community celebration   b. community race   c. downhill race

A Second Look at Vocabulary

Complete the sentences. Use the words from the first exercise.

1. You can protect your eyes by wearing _____.

2. The white snow makes the _____ from the sun even brighter.

3. In _____ races, skiers can go faster than 40 miles an hour.

4. People come to the town to enjoy the food and dancing at the _____.

5. Thousands of _____ travel to Steamboat Springs and Aspen each year.

6. The _____ in the mountains is beautiful in winter and summer.

7. Skis made from _____ are strong, but they bend when needed.

Colorado

Understanding the Reading

Choose the best answer.

_____ **1.** Skiing began to become popular in the United States
   a. in the 1800s.
   b. after World War I.
   c. after World War II.

_____ **2.** In the United States, skiing began in
   a. Steamboat Springs.
   b. Aspen.
   c. Boulder.

_____ **3.** Unlike skiers in the 1930s and 1940s, today's skiers
   a. wear business shirts and plain sweaters.
   b. use wooden skis.
   c. wear colorful clothing, ski pants, and parkas.

Reading between the Lines

Look carefully at the reading. Mark each statement _T_ for _true_ or _F_ for _false_.

_____ **1.** Before World War I, Americans had to go to Europe to ski.

_____ **2.** Norwegians introduced skiing into America.

_____ **3.** Even today, few good skiers go to Colorado for skiing.

Why Did It Happen?

Match the sentence parts.

_____ **1.** Colorado has mountains,

_____ **2.** Fiberglass skis were invented,

_____ **3.** Skiers wear parkas

_____ **4.** Ski lifts were invented,

a. so skiing is easier.

b. so it is easier for skiers to get up mountains.

c. so it is good for skiing.

d. so that they will be warm.

What Do You Think?
Discuss these questions.

1. Do you or would you like to ski? Why or why not?

2. Do you think downhill skiing is too dangerous? Explain your answer.

A Last Look
Write about one of these topics.

1. Many people go downhill skiing. Others go cross-country skiing. Learn about these two types of skiing and write a comparison.

2. Learn about the kinds of equipment needed for downhill skiing. Describe the equipment, and explain how skiers use it.

Idaho

Thinking about the Picture
1. Where are these men working?
2. What are they looking for?
3. What is it like to be a miner?

Gold and Silver

Mineral resources have been important in the history of Idaho. Many of its early settlers were looking for silver or gold. In 1860, Elias Pierce discovered gold in central Idaho. A "gold rush" began. People who search for gold are called prospectors. Thousands of them rushed to the area. A few made a fortune. Most did not.

Prospectors built many towns in Idaho during the gold rush. By 1863, about 25,000 people had come to search for gold. Between 1860 and 1866, prospectors mined gold worth about $20 million. In the 1870s and 1880s, miners found silver, lead, copper, and other metals. The population grew quickly. Idaho became a state in 1890.

Lead and silver were found in northern Idaho in 1883. A famous mining district developed around the town of Coeur d'Alene. Wallace, a nearby town, calls itself the Silver Capital of the World. Once, about one-fourth of the nation's silver and lead came from mines there. More than one billion ounces of silver were produced. Today only two silver mines are working.

Over time, silver and gold mining declined in Idaho. Some mines ran out of ore. The government controlled the price of gold. The price of silver dropped. When the cost of mining went up, some mines had to close. Many mining towns were abandoned. They became "ghost towns."

One famous ghost town is Silver City, near Boise. It was a busy town from about 1866 until the 1930s. About 700 Chinese worked in the Silver City mines. A huge silver crystal weighing 500 pounds was found there. During the 1940s, however, the last mines in Silver City closed. Tourists visit Silver City to imagine life there long ago.

The days of the gold rush are over, but minerals are still important in Idaho's economy. Today, phosphate is valuable. It is used in fertilizer.

A First Look at Vocabulary

Match each term with its meaning.

_____	**1.** minerals	a.	place where a mineral is found
_____	**2.** gold rush	b.	something that helps plants grow
_____	**3.** prospector	c.	a lot of money
_____	**4.** fortune	d.	solid materials formed in the earth
_____	**5.** mined	e.	business system; way of making money
_____	**6.** declined	f.	many people hurrying to look for gold
_____	**7.** economy	g.	person who looks for gold or other minerals
_____	**8.** ghost town	h.	dug into the earth for minerals
_____	**9.** fertilizer	i.	town where people no longer live
_____	**10.** deposit	j.	became less

A Second Look at Vocabulary

Complete the sentences. Use the words from the first exercise.

1. When the amount of gold in the ground _____, many miners had to find other work.

2. When a prospector found a _____ of silver, he dug it out of the ground.

3. A _____ might search for years and never find gold.

4. Gold, silver, lead, and copper are all _____ found in Idaho.

5. Idaho's _____ depends on tourists and farms as well as mining.

6. A few prospectors found gold and made a _____.

7. Some towns became _____ after the mines closed.

8. Phosphate from Idaho is used to make _____ for crops.

9. People raced to Idaho during the _____ and hoped to become rich.

10. Prospectors used shovels and other hand tools as they _____ for gold in the earth.

Idaho

Understanding the Reading

Choose the best answer.

_____ **1.** In 1860, people rushed to what is now Idaho because
   a. silver was discovered in Silver City and Coeur d'Alene.
   b. Elias Pierce discovered gold there.
   c. it was discovered that phosphate makes good fertilizer.

_____ **2.** Between 1860 and 1890, the population of Idaho
   a. changed very little.
   b. increased slowly.
   c. increased rapidly.

_____ **3.** Some mines closed because
   a. the price of gold declined and the cost of mining went up.
   b. the price of gold went up and the cost of mining declined.
   c. the government controlled the price of gold.

_____ **4.** Which is true of mining in Idaho today?
   a. None of the old mines are still producing silver.
   b. Mining is still important to Idaho.
   c. Only phosphate is still important to Idaho's economy.

Fact or Opinion?

Mark each statement *F* for *fact* or *O* for *opinion*.

_____ **1.** There was a gold rush to Idaho in the 1860s.

_____ **2.** People were foolish to join the gold rush.

_____ **3.** Tourists are the reason Silver City still exists.

When Did It Happen?

Write numbers to put the events in the order they happened.

_____ Idaho became a state.

_____ A gold rush began in central Idaho.

_____ The last mines in Silver City closed.

_____ Prospectors found lead and silver in northern Idaho.

What Do You Think?
Discuss these questions.

1. Would you like to visit a ghost town? Why?
2. If you had lived during the 1860s, would you have joined the gold rush? Why or why not?

A Last Look
Write about one of these topics.

1. How did the discovery of gold and silver change Idaho and the West? Were all the changes good? Explain.
2. How do you think the miners felt when the mines closed? What do you think happened to them?

Idaho

Kansas

Thinking about the Picture

1. Describe this home. What do you think it is made from?

2. What can you tell about where this home is?

3. What do you think the man's life was like?

Settling the Prairie

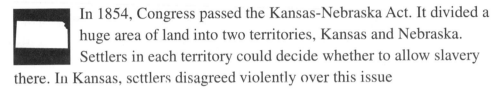

In 1854, Congress passed the Kansas-Nebraska Act. It divided a huge area of land into two territories, Kansas and Nebraska. Settlers in each territory could decide whether to allow slavery there. In Kansas, settlers disagreed violently over this issue

Kansas Territory was soon the center of a bloody battle over slavery. Anti-slavery forces sent in new settlers. Pro-slavery people voted illegally. Both sides raided the other's towns and burned buildings. People began to call the territory "Bleeding Kansas." Between 1854 and 1861, more than 200 people died. At last, Kansas entered the Union in 1861 as a free state.

After the Civil War ended in 1865, many people settled in Kansas. The Homestead Act of 1862 encouraged new settlers. It offered 160 acres of land for $10. To own the land, the settler would have build a house, live there, and farm for five years. The federal government also gave free land to railroad companies. Other settlers were black Americans from the South. In the 1870s and 1880s, thousands moved to Kansas even though life there was difficult and dangerous.

Settlers and Native Americans fought over land. Families lived far apart. Homesteads were miles away from doctors and supplies. The Kansas weather was hard. Winters were cold and snowy. Summers were hot and dusty. Often there was little rain, so crops died. Prairie fires burned down farms. Grasshoppers ate crops. Western Kansas had few trees to supply wood for houses. Settlers built houses out of sod—large blocks of prairie grass and soil. They burned dried buffalo and cow manure for heat.

In the 1870s, new farm machinery made life easier for Kansas farmers. Immigrants from Russia brought a new kind of wheat. It grew well in the Kansas climate. The state became the "Breadbasket of America." It is still the largest producer of wheat in the United States.

Kansas

A First Look at Vocabulary

Choose the best definition for each word in bold type.

_____ **1.** Families wanted to start farms on the Kansas **prairie.**
       a. hills   b. flat grassland   c. river valley

_____ **2.** In 1854, Congress created the Kansas **territory.**
       a. independent country   b. state   c. land that's not a state

_____ **3.** People were either **violently** for slavery or violently against it.
       a. with very strong feeling   b. illegally   c. without thinking

_____ **4.** A voter acted **illegally** when he voted twice in one election.
       a. carelessly   b. against the law   c. openly

_____ **5.** During the Civil War, soldiers **raided** towns for food and supplies.
       a. ran away from   b. looked for   c. quickly attacked

_____ **6.** The settlers lived in a **homestead** near the river.
       a. wagon   b. boat   c. land with a home

_____ **7.** The settlers went into town for **supplies.**
       a. things needed to live   b. free land   c. voting on issues

_____ **8.** Houses were made from **sod** that was cut out of the prairie.
       a. grass with roots and soil   b. bricks made from mud   c. wood

A Second Look at Vocabulary

Complete the sentences. Use the words from the first exercise.

1. Settlers would argue _____ about slavery.

2. When a town was _____, it might be set on fire.

3. Kansas was a _____, but people wanted it to become a state.

4. Cutting _____ from the prairie to build homes was hard work.

5. Settlers might live on their _____ for months without seeing anyone.

6. The grass of the _____ was thick and green that spring.

7. They grew most of what they needed and bought the few _____ they needed.

8. Sometimes protestors act _____ even when they stay peaceful.

Kansas

Understanding the Reading

Choose the best answer.

_____ 1. The Kansas-Nebraska Act of 1854
   a. allowed settlers to decide whether or not to allow slavery.
   b. offered 160 acres for $10.
   c. gave free land to railroads.

_____ 2. Before the Civil War, the people of Kansas
   a. argued over who owned the land.
   b. began raising Russian wheat.
   c. fought bloody battles over slavery.

_____ 3. The Homestead Act
   a. brought many new settlers to Kansas.
   b. divided the territory into Kansas and Nebraska.
   c. helped settlers who lost their crops to fires or grasshoppers.

_____ 4. Life on the Kansas prairie was difficult because
   a. the land was so expensive.
   b. the land was hard to farm without slaves.
   c. fire, too little rain, and grasshoppers destroyed crops.

Why Did It Happen?

Match the sentence parts.

_____ 1. Kansas became known as "Bleeding Kansas" because

_____ 2. After 1862, many people came to Kansas because

_____ 3. Settlers built their homes from sod because

_____ 4. Kansas became the "Breadbasket of America" because

_____ 5. African Americans came to Kansas because

a. of the Homestead Act.

b. wheat from Russia grew well in Kansas.

c. people fought and died over slavery.

d. life was hard for freed slaves in the South.

e. there were few trees.

Kansas

115

What Do You Think?
Discuss these questions.

1. Life was hard and dangerous in the Kansas Territory. Why do you think people settled there?

2. The federal government let the people of Kansas Territory choose if they wanted slavery there. As a result, violent and bloody battles were fought. Do you think the government's plan was a good one? Why or why not?

A Last Look
Write about one of these topics.

1. Would you like to live on a wheat farm in Kansas today? Why or why not?

2. What do you think a Native American would think about the events that happened in Kansas in the 1800s?

Montana

Thinking about the Picture

1. What kind of clothes are these Native Americans wearing? Describe them.
2. What are these people doing?

Powwows

Native American culture is important in Montana. The state has seven reservations, which represent 11 different tribes. Many reservations have museums that display their rich traditions. They also preserve historic sites such as the Little Bighorn Battlefield. Some of the most colorful events are the celebrations called powwows. During the summer, many tribal communities in Montana hold powwows.

A powwow includes parades, horse races, and dances. Some are open to the public, but they are not for tourists. For Native Americans, they are like huge family reunions. People come to dance and to see friends and family.

One of the largest Indian celebrations in Montana is the Crow Fair Powwow and Rodeo. It is held on the Crow reservation each year in August. The Crow Fair is sometimes called "The Tepee Capital of the World." Plains Indians come from other states and from Canada and Mexico. They set up more than a thousand tepees along the Little Bighorn River. At the center of the camp is the dance area.

A day at the Crow Fair begins with a parade of trucks, cars, and horses. Men, women, and children wear colorful traditional clothing. They ride on horses with decorated saddles and bright blankets. Later in the day, there is an all-Indian rodeo, with cowboys from many states.

Dancing goes on in the central arena. Everyone can take part in the intertribal dance. Other dances are done only by men or by women. There are several categories of dancing: Traditional, Fancy, Grass, and Jingle Dress. Each has its own steps and costumes. Dance costumes include buckskin dresses, feather headdresses, and bells on the ankles. Groups of drummers accompany each type of dance. Both dancers and drummers compete to outdo each other. But for Native Americans, a powwow is mainly a time for having fun and sharing traditions.

A First Look at Vocabulary

Match each term with its meaning.

_____ **1.** reservation   a. field or area where an event takes place

_____ **2.** preserve   b. type

_____ **3.** tribal   c. seat used on a horse for riding

_____ **4.** reunion   d. with added items to make it prettier

_____ **5.** tepee   e. protect

_____ **6.** camp   f. land set aside for Native Americans

_____ **7.** decorated   g. a coming back together

_____ **8.** saddle   h. belonging to a tribe

_____ **9.** arena   i. a Native American tent

_____ **10.** category   j. an outdoor place where tents are set up

A Second Look at Vocabulary

Complete the sentences. Use the words from the first exercise.

1. At the center of the camp was the _____ where the dancing and other ceremonies were held.

2. Most dancers are not skilled in every _____ of dance.

3. The Crow, Dakota, and other _____ groups hold powwows.

4. Each tribe wants to _____ its traditions so they will be remembered in the years to come.

5. The Crow make their own laws on their _____.

6. Many people have a family _____ each year when relatives visit.

7. Once, each Crow family lived in a _____ for part of every year.

8. The _____ contained more than a thousand tepees.

9. The dancing costumes may be _____ with drawings and feathers.

10. Although people sometimes ride without a _____, it is more comfortable to have a seat when riding a horse.

Understanding the Reading

Choose the best answer.

_____ 1. Native American culture is important in Montana because
   a. most of Montana's population is Native Americans.
   b. 11 tribes preserve their traditions on seven reservations.
   c. powwows bring many tourists to Montana.

_____ 2. The Crow Fair is called "The Tepee Capital of the World"
   a. because more than a thousand tepees are set up.
   b. because everyone stays in a tepee during the powwow.
   c. so that tourists know this is a Native American event.

_____ 3. The Crow Fair
   a. lasts just one day during the summer.
   b. is for Crow Indians only.
   c. has a parade, an all-Indian rodeo, and dances in the arena.

Fact or Opinion?

Mark each statement _F_ for _fact_ or _O_ for _opinion_.

_____ 1. The Crow Fair is the best powwow in Montana.

_____ 2. Native Americans go to powwows to have fun and see friends.

_____ 3. Powwows help Native Americans preserve their cultures.

Where's the Idea?

These are main ideas from the reading. Write the number of the paragraph where you find each idea.

_____ Many events take place each day during the Crow Fair.

_____ For Native Americans, powwows are like family reunions.

_____ Native Americans in Montana try to preserve their culture.

_____ Dancing takes place in the central arena.

_____ The Crow Fair is one of the largest Native American celebrations.

What Do You Think?

Discuss these questions.

1. Would you like to attend a powwow? Why or why not?

2. Is it important to keep traditions alive? Why or why not?

A Last Look

Write about one of these topics.

1. Tribal groups of Montana include the Blackfoot, Crow, Cree, Chippewa, Flathead, Salish, Kootenai, Assiniboine, Gros Ventre, Sioux, and Cheyenne. Learn about one of these groups. Where is the group's reservation? How many people are in the group? Where do they live? Where did this group live before they had a reservation?

2. Why do you think Native Americans have reservations? Do you think this is a good idea? How do you think Native Americans feel about living on a reservation?

Montana

Nebraska

Thinking about the Picture
1. Who is the man on the right? Why is he important?
2. Why do children get in trouble? What may happen to them if they get in trouble with the police?

Girls and Boys Town

A village near Omaha, Nebraska, is the national center for programs that help young people throughout the country. The village is called Boys Town. It was once known as the "City of Little Men." Since 1979, Boys Town has welcomed girls, too. Its programs are now called "Girls and Boys Town." About half its residents are girls.

The program helps children and teenagers who are abused, homeless, or neglected. It also helps young people who are in various kinds of trouble. Juvenile courts, schools, and social workers send young people here. There are schools, housing, a career center, and places for activities.

Father Edward Flanagan, a Roman Catholic priest, started Boys Town. He was born in Ireland in 1886 and came to the United States in 1904. He decided to help boys who broke the law before they became "lost men." Father Flanagan believed all boys could become good citizens if they had the right home and education.

In 1917, Father Flanagan borrowed $90 and rented an old house in Omaha. Two nuns helped him care for five boys who were in trouble with the law. Soon the courts sent more boys to the home. Others came because they had nowhere else to go. Father Flanagan gave them a home, understanding, and education. He helped them turn their lives around.

More boys continued to arrive. Father Flanagan moved Boys Town to a farm. Many of the boys had trouble in public school, so he started his own school. Father Flanagan believed it was better to educate troubled teens than to send them to prison. In 1948 he died suddenly of a heart attack.

Girls and Boys Town cares for thousands of boys and girls a year in Omaha. It has set up youth centers around the nation. A telephone hotline is available 24 hours a day for children and their parents.

A First Look at Vocabulary

Choose the best definition for each word in bold type.

_____ **1.** Girls and Boys Town has special **programs** to help young people.
   a. people   b. money   c. plans and activities

_____ **2.** The **residents** are boys and girls who have had trouble.
   a. people who live there   b. teachers   c. people who pay

_____ **3.** Some of the boys and girls have been **abused** by their parents.
   a. protected   b. hurt   c. left

_____ **4.** Children who are **homeless** are given a place to live.
   a. without a home   b. new to the home   c. away from home

_____ **5.** **Neglected** children need love and attention paid to them.
   a. beaten   b. not taken care of   c. angry

_____ **6.** A **juvenile** who has broken the law may go to the center.
   a. young mother   b. adult   c. young person

_____ **7.** A **social worker** talks to the young people and tries to help.
   a. teacher   b. person trained to help   c. police officer

_____ **8.** A young person who is scared can call a **hotline** to get help.
   a. business phone   b. home phone   c. emergency phone

A Second Look at Vocabulary

Complete the sentences. Use the words from the first exercise.

1. _____ children lived on the street and slept in cardboard boxes.

2. Most of the _____ of the center like living there.

3. A _____ needs to be cared for by adults.

4. Some _____ teach children how to work together.

5. Children can use the _____ to call for help day or night.

6. A _____ may try to help a troubled family.

7. Children who are _____ may lack food, clothing, medicine, or love.

8. Children who are _____ may be hurt mentally and physically.

Nebraska

Understanding the Reading

Choose the best answer.

_____ **1.** Girls and Boys Town offers programs to help
   a. young people who want to go to college.
   b. young people who are abused, homeless, or neglected.
   c. young people who are Catholic and live in Nebraska.

_____ **2.** Boys Town was started
   a. by Nebraska social workers.
   b. as a home for boys and girls.
   c. in an old house in Omaha, Nebraska.

_____ **3.** Girls and Boys Town
   a. now has youth centers around the country.
   b. is still run by Father Flanagan.
   c. has fewer children today because fewer children need help.

Reading between the Lines

Look carefully at the reading. Mark each statement _T_ for _true_ or _F_ for _false_.

_____ **1.** Father Flanagan would agree that there are no bad boys, only boys who need help.

_____ **2.** Girls and Boys Town has fewer girls since girls need less help.

_____ **3.** Boys Town moved out of Omaha because some boys are dangerous.

_____ **4.** Children can always get help at Girls and Boys Town.

When Did It Happen?

Write numbers to put the events in the order they happened.

_____ Boys Town started taking girls as well as boys.

_____ Father Flanagan rented a house in Omaha.

_____ Boys Town moved to a farm outside of Omaha.

_____ Father Flanagan died.

What Do You Think?
Discuss these questions.

1. Father Flanagan believed children who break the law need help, not prison. Do you agree? Explain your reasons.
2. What is the biggest reason that young people get into trouble?

A Last Look
Write about one of these topics.

1. What is the best way to help young people stay out of trouble?
2. What programs does your community have to help children and teenagers?

Nevada

Thinking about the Picture

1. What kind of business is pictured here?
2. Would you want to get married in this kind of place? Why or why not?

Las Vegas

Las Vegas, Nevada, is one of the fastest-growing cities in the United States. About 16,000 people a year move there. About 36 million tourists visit it every year. It is a favorite city for conventions. Yet Las Vegas is in the hot, dry desert. Why do so many people want to visit or live there?

Some people go to Las Vegas to get married. More than 100,000 couples marry in " Vegas" every year. Nevada state laws have made it "the wedding capital of the world." There is no waiting period or blood test to get a marriage license. Couples can choose from 100 wedding chapels. Some chapels provide flowers, music, photographs, and limousines. People also go to Las Vegas for divorces. They need to live in Nevada only six weeks to get a divorce there.

Gambling is another attraction. " Vegas" is famous for its gambling casinos. Bright neon signs light up the outside of casinos and hotels. The casinos are open 24 hours a day. Guests hope to win a lot of money by playing games such as blackjack. Others risk their money in slot machines. One hotel has 3,000 slot machines. Even the airport is full of them.

Las Vegas has some of the largest hotels in the world. The MGM Grand Hotel/Casino has emerald-green towers 30 stories high. It has more than 5,000 rooms. Many Las Vegas hotels follow a theme, or idea. The Luxor Hotel imitates ancient Egypt. Caesar's Palace follows the theme of ancient Rome. Entertainment goes on all day and all night. Visitors can see and hear famous performers. Spectacular shows feature dancers in eye-catching costumes.

People decide to live in Las Vegas for many reasons. Nevada has no state income tax. That appeals to retired people. Younger people move to Las Vegas to work in the tourist industry or on the nearby military bases.

Nevada

A First Look at Vocabulary

Match each term with its meaning.

_____ **1.** convention   a. risking money on a game

_____ **2.** desert   b. very old

_____ **3.** license   c. copy

_____ **4.** chapel   d. place where people gamble

_____ **5.** divorce   e. large meeting

_____ **6.** gambling   f. land that is very dry

_____ **7.** casino   g. legal end of a marriage

_____ **8.** imitate   h. small church

_____ **9.** ancient   i. paper that lets you do something

A Second Look at Vocabulary

Choose the best answer to complete each sentence.

_____ **1.** Some married couples end their marriage with a ____.
   a. divorce   b. license   c. industry

_____ **2.** To start a business, you must first get a ____ from the city.
   a. license   b. divorce   c. hotel

_____ **3.** ____ Egypt was a powerful nation thousands of years ago.
   a. Modern   b. Spectacular   c. Ancient

_____ **4.** People may go to a ____ to learn about business.
   a. casino   b. convention   c. chapel

_____ **5.** A hotel ____ interesting places to make people want to stay there.
   a. appeals   b. imitates   c. permits

_____ **6.** Most people who go to Las Vegas for ____ lose money.
   a. license   b. convention   c. gambling

_____ **7.** The ____ around Las Vegas is dry and very hot in the summers.
   a. casino   b. mountains   c. desert

_____ **8.** In almost any ____, you can gamble all night long.
   a. casino   b. convention   c. show

_____ **9.** Many people get married in a ____ because they are religious.
   a. convention   b. chapel   c. wedding

Understanding the Reading

Choose the best answer.

_____ **1.** Las Vegas, Nevada,
   a. is most famous for education and business.
   b. is one of the fastest growing cities in the United States.
   c. has a comfortable climate.

_____ **2.** Nevada state laws
   a. make it easy to get married in Las Vegas.
   b. make it illegal to gamble after 12 o'clock at night.
   c. allow people who do not live in Nevada to get a divorce there.

_____ **3.** Most tourists come to Las Vegas
   a. to gamble, to swim and surf, and to enjoy the entertainment.
   b. to gamble, to ski, and to get married.
   c. to gamble, to go to conventions, and to see famous performers.

_____ **4.** Las Vegas has
   a. some of the largest hotels in the world.
   b. one of the highest income taxes in the United States.
   c. the fewest divorces of any city in the country.

Reading between the Lines

Look carefully at the reading. Mark each statement _T_ for _true_ or _F_ for _false_.

_____ **1.** Las Vegas is a good place for young people who want jobs.

_____ **2.** Las Vegas is not popular with people who retire.

_____ **3.** People can get a divorce in Nevada after just six days.

Fact or Opinion?

Mark each statement _F_ for _fact_ or _O_ for _opinion_.

_____ **1.** Las Vegas is a great place to live.

_____ **2.** Many people go to Las Vegas to get married.

_____ **3.** No one can get rich by gambling.

What Do You Think?
Discuss these questions.

1. Why is gambling so popular with so many people?

2. Do you think it is a good idea or a bad one to let people get married and divorced quickly?

3. Why do people want to stay in hotels that imitate ancient countries? Why do they watch shows where performers dress in spectacular costumes?

A Last Look
Write about one of these topics.

1. Learn about the history of Las Vegas. Write a summary of how it got started.

2. Would you like to live in Las Vegas? Why or why not?

Nevada

North Dakota

Thinking about the Picture
1. What are these animals?
2. Where would you go to see these animals?
3. Why do people enjoy seeing wild animals?

The Buffalo

 A huge statue in Jamestown, North Dakota, honors the buffalo. The statue is three stories high and weighs 60 tons. It reminds visitors how important the buffalo was in the American West.

Once, millions of buffalo roamed the prairies. Plains Indians had hunted them for centuries. They used almost every part of the animal. They ate the meat and made the skins into clothes and blankets. Skins also covered the cone-shaped tents called tepees. Bones and hooves became tools and containers.

What Americans call a "buffalo" is not like the buffalo of Asia or Africa. Its correct name is "American bison." It is North America's largest land mammal. An adult male weighs up to 3,000 pounds (about 1,400 kilos). It stands $5^1/_2$ to $6^1/_2$ feet tall at the shoulder. Both males and females have horns. Thick dark brown hair protects them in cold winters.

At first, the Plains Indians hunted buffalo on foot. In the 1500s, Spanish explorers brought horses to North America. After that, the Plains Indians hunted on horseback. When the Europeans arrived, there may have been 60 million buffalo on the plains. They traveled in huge herds. It was easy to hunt and kill hundreds of animals at a time.

As settlers moved west in the 1800s, they killed millions of buffalo. Unlike the Native Americans, they did not hunt carefully. Sometimes they took only the hides. They also shot buffalo that blocked train lines or damaged farms. Tourists came by train to shoot buffalo for sport. By 1894, there were only about 500 buffalo left in the United States.

Conservationists, including President Theodore Roosevelt, wanted to save the bison. Buffalo hunting was made illegal. The government started reserves to protect the herds. Today there are hundreds of thousands of buffalo in the U.S. They live in parks and reserves, and on private land.

A First Look at Vocabulary

Match each term with its meaning.

_____ **1.** conservationist   a. animal's outer covering

_____ **2.** century   b. hard bottom part of some animals' feet

_____ **3.** skin   c. place set aside for some purpose

_____ **4.** hooves   d. large group of animals

_____ **5.** mammal   e. hard pointed things on some mammals' heads

_____ **6.** horn   f. 100 years

_____ **7.** herd   g. someone who tries to protect natural things

_____ **8.** reserve   h. animal with warm blood that nurses its young with milk

A Second Look at Vocabulary

Choose the best answer to complete each sentence.

_____ **1.** _____ wanted to save the buffalo and other animals from dying out.

    a. Conservationists   b. Settlers   c. Explorers

_____ **2.** A _____ ago, the great buffalo herds were gone from the prairie.

    a. ton   b. million   c. century

_____ **3.** The buffalo can run for many miles on its hard _____ and strong legs.

    a. skin   b. horns   c. hooves

_____ **4.** The _____ are pointed and help the buffalo fight off wolves.

    a. skin   b. horns   c. hooves

_____ **5.** Native Americans used the _____ of buffalo to make tepees.

    a. skin   b. horns   c. hooves

_____ **6.** _____ were set up where buffalo could live without being hunted.

    a. Prairies   b. Reserves   c. Farms

_____ **7.** Besides the buffalo, other _____ that lived on the prairie were wolves, bears, and coyotes.

    a. mammals   b. horses   c. bison

_____ **8.** Buffalo lived in huge _____ of hundreds and thousands of animals.

    a. horns   b. herds   c. plains

Understanding the Reading

Choose the best answer.

_____ 1. Hundreds of years ago,
  a. millions of buffalo roamed the prairies.
  b. the Spanish brought buffalo to North America.
  c. buffalo lived on large reserves.

_____ 2. Plains Indians
  a. used almost every part of the buffalo.
  b. killed too many buffalo.
  c. killed buffalo that damaged their villages.

_____ 3. Settlers killed millions of buffalo
  a. but used most of the animal.
  b. to help the Native Americans protect their farms.
  c. so that only 500 were left by 1894.

_____ 4. The government started reserves for buffalo
  a. and allowed people to go there and shoot buffalo for sport.
  b. and today there are hundreds of thousands of buffalo.
  c. but doesn't protect them any more.

Alike or Different?

Complete the chart to compare and contrast how Native Americans and settlers used the buffalo.

	Native Americans	**Settlers**	**Alike or Different?**
Why did they kill buffalo?			
How many buffalo did they kill?			
How did they affect the herds of buffalo?			

What Do You Think?
Discuss these questions.

1. Why didn't the settlers worry about killing all of the buffalo?

2. Why did conservationists decide that the buffalo should be saved? Was this a good idea? Why or why not?

3. Why is the buffalo one of the symbols of the American West?

A Last Look
Write about one of these topics.

1. Conservationists are now trying to save these animals: gray wolf, Florida panther, grizzly bear, and bighorn sheep. Learn about one of these animals. Explain where they live, why they are endangered, and what can be done to save them.

2. Today, many buffalo are raised on ranches. What do ranchers do with the buffalo? How hard is it to raise buffalo on a ranch?

South Dakota

Thinking about the Picture

1. These heads are carved from what?
2. If the larger trees are 30 feet tall, how tall is each head?
3. Who are the people in this sculpture?

Monuments in Stone

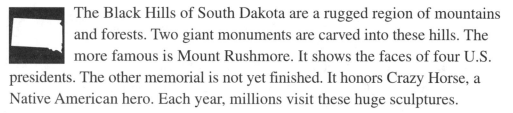

The Black Hills of South Dakota are a rugged region of mountains and forests. Two giant monuments are carved into these hills. The more famous is Mount Rushmore. It shows the faces of four U.S. presidents. The other memorial is not yet finished. It honors Crazy Horse, a Native American hero. Each year, millions visit these huge sculptures.

Mount Rushmore was the idea of a South Dakota historian. The sculptor Gutzon Borglum was chosen to carve it. He was already famous for huge works in stone. Planners chose four great presidents: Washington, Jefferson, Lincoln, and Theodore Roosevelt. Washington and Jefferson stand for America's beginnings. Lincoln kept the nation together. Roosevelt oversaw expansion and conservation. Their faces are carved high on a solid granite cliff. Each head is about 60 feet tall, about as high as a five-story building.

Work on carving the monument began in 1927. The U.S. government paid for most of the work. Borglum died in March 1941, with the project almost finished. His son Lincoln completed it the same year.

The monument to Crazy Horse was the idea of a Lakota chief, Henry Standing Bear. He said, "My fellow chiefs and I would like the white man to know that the red man has great heroes too." Crazy Horse was an Oglala Sioux leader who fought against the takeover of Indian lands. In 1876, he and other Sioux warriors defeated Colonel George A. Custer and his soldiers in a famous battle. Crazy Horse later surrendered and was killed while a prisoner.

The sculptor Korczak Ziolkowski began work on the statue in 1948. It is carved into a cliff about 17 miles from Mount Rushmore. The design shows Crazy Horse pointing to the Black Hills. Ziolkowski died in 1982, but his family and others continued the work. The head of Crazy Horse was finished in June 1998. It is nearly 88 feet tall. When finished, the whole statue will be 641 feet long and 563 feet high.

South Dakota

A First Look at Vocabulary

Choose the best definition for each word in bold type.

_____ 1. The **rugged** Black Hills are a steep and rocky region.
  a. low and round b. high and big   c. rough and uneven

_____ 2. A **historian** can tell you about the Battle of the Little Big Horn.
  a. artist   b. someone who studies the past c. someone who studies government

_____ 3. Has **expansion** of the United States ended, or will more states join?
  a. government   b. growth   c. war

_____ 4. The rock of the monument is almost all **granite.**
  a. pieces   b. white and yellow   c. type of hard rock

_____ 5. The **cliff** is steep and has few trees or bushes on it.
  a. steep rock face b. low place between hills   c. flat top of hill

_____ 6. **Carving** monuments like these takes many years.
  a. painting   b. planning   c. cutting

_____ 7. The Sioux **defeated** and killed George Custer and his army.
  a. captured   b. won a victory over   c. hated

_____ 8. Crazy Horse **surrendered** because he knew he could not win.
  a. gave up   b. began a war   c. stopped

A Second Look at Vocabulary

Complete the sentences. Use the words from the first exercise.

1. The _____ is steep, so the workers had to be careful not to fall.

2. Crazy Horse _____ to the U.S. Army and gave up his guns.

3. A _____ wrote a book about the Battle of the Little Big Horn.

4. Custer's army was _____, and not a soldier lived.

5. The _____ of the cliff is very hard and good for carving.

6. Many different tools were used for _____ the giant heads.

7. The last _____ of the United States happened when Alaska and Hawaii became states.

Understanding the Reading

Choose the best answer.

_____ **1.** Mount Rushmore has the faces of Washington, Jefferson,
   a. Lincoln, and Theodore Roosevelt.
   b. Lincoln, and Franklin Roosevelt.
   c. Lincoln, and George W. Bush.

_____ **2.** Crazy Horse was a
   a. leader of the U.S. Army.
   b. sculptor who carved a statue in the Black Hills.
   c. Oglala Sioux leader who defeated George Custer in a battle.

_____ **3.** Mount Rushmore and the Crazy Horse monument
   a. were both finished in the same year.
   b. were carved into cliffs just 17 miles apart.
   c. were begun in the same year.

_____ **4.** The Mount Rushmore monument mostly was paid for by
   a. the state of South Dakota.
   b. the U.S. government.
   c. Gutzon Borglum and his family.

_____ **5.** The Crazy Horse monument
   a. is in the Black Hills.
   b. was carved to honor George Custer.
   c. is much smaller than the Rushmore Monument.

What Do You Think?

Discuss these questions.

1. Were the right presidents chosen for the Mount Rushmore monument? Why or why not? Who would you choose?

2. What modern American would you choose for a monument? Explain your choice.

A Last Look

Write about one of these topics.

1. If you were building a giant sculpture of a great person from your native country, who would you choose? Why?

2. How were the giant figures of the two monuments carved? What tools were used?

Alike or Different?

Complete the chart to compare and contrast the two monuments.

	Mount Rushmore Monument	**Crazy Horse Monument**	**Alike or Different?**
Where is it?			
How many men are shown?			
Is it finished?			

Utah

Thinking about the Picture

1. These people are not swimming. They are floating without any effort. Where can people do this?
2. What sports and outdoor activities do you enjoy?

The Great Salt Lake

In North America, the last great ice age ended about 12,000 years ago. At that time, a huge lake covered much of western Utah. Geologists call it Lake Bonneville. The ancient lake spread over almost 20,000 square miles. It was about 1,000 feet deep. Many animals lived in the lake or near it. As the weather became warmer and drier, the lake water evaporated. Lake Bonneville began to shrink. What is left is the Great Salt Lake. The rest of the old lake bed is flat desert.

Great Salt Lake is the largest lake in North America west of the Mississippi River. The water level varies, depending on the local rainfall. Usually, the lake covers about 1,700 square miles. It is one of the saltiest bodies of water in the world. Only the Dead Sea in the Middle East is saltier. On average, the oceans are 3.5 percent salt. Parts of Great Salt Lake are as much as 27 percent salt. Rivers flow into the lake, bringing minerals and salts, but the lake has no outlet. Water evaporates from the surface, leaving salts behind.

Only a few kinds of life can live in this salty water. They include blue-green algae, bacteria, and tiny brine shrimp. Brine flies eat the bacteria and algae. Great Salt Lake is paradise for bird-watchers. Many migrating birds stop here. They build nests on islands in the lake. They eat brine shrimp and insects.

Since the 1800s, this unusual region has attracted many visitors. Swimmers have a rare experience. The very salty water is buoyant—it supports them. Without trying, they can float on the surface in parts of the lake.

Great Salt Lake is valuable in other ways. It supplies salts and other minerals, such as magnesium, potash, and lithium. These are used in farming and industry. Brine shrimp and their eggs go into food for aquarium fish. In 1903, a railway across the lake was built on a raised wooden platform. In 1959, a rock-filled causeway, or raised highway, replaced it. The causeway split the lake into two sections, with different levels of saltiness.

A First Look at Vocabulary

Match each term with its meaning.

_____ **1.** ice age   a. beautiful, happy place

_____ **2.** geologist   b. changes

_____ **3.** evaporated   c. able to keep something floating

_____ **4.** varies   d. scientist who studies rocks and other earth materials

_____ **5.** outlet   e. traveling from place to place

_____ **6.** paradise   f. a time when ice spread across the earth

_____ **7.** migrating   g. way out

_____ **8.** buoyant   h. dried up

A Second Look at Vocabulary

Choose the best answer to complete each sentence.

_____ **1.** The number of birds ____ because the amount of food changes.

    a. supports   b. varies   c. evaporates

_____ **2.** The ____ studied the rocks and soil of Utah.

    a. geologist   b. hunter   c. bacteria

_____ **3.** During the ____, large sheets of ice covered much of North America.

    a. paradise   b. aquarium   c. ice age

_____ **4.** ____ birds need a place to stop and rest before traveling on.

    a. Migrating   b. Resting   c. Buoyant

_____ **5.** The lake is smaller because water has ____.

    a. migrated   b. varied   c. evaporated

_____ **6.** A lake with an ____ has a river or stream flowing out of it.

    a. outlet   b. aquarium   c. island

_____ **7.** Fresh water can keep some things floating, but salt water is even more ____.

    a. unusual   b. buoyant   c. common

_____ **8.** Birds must think Great Salt Lake is ____ because there is so much food.

    a. causeway   b. paradise   c. desert

Understanding the Reading

Choose the best answer.

_____ **1.** Great Salt Lake is
    a. much smaller than Lake Bonneville was.
    b. much larger than Lake Bonneville was.
    c. about the same size as Lake Bonneville was.

_____ **2.** Great Salt Lake is very salty because
    a. no water can enter the lake.
    b. rivers flow into the lake.
    c. water cannot flow out of the lake.

_____ **3.** Many kinds of birds are found at Great Salt Lake because
    a. many kinds of fish and other animals live in the lake.
    b. brine shrimp and insects are a good source of food for the birds.
    c. the blue-green algae are food for birds.

_____ **4.** The water level of Great Salt Lake depends upon
    a. how much water is taken away for industry.
    b. how much water is used for farming.
    c. how much rain falls in the region.

Why Did It Happen?

Match the sentence parts.

_____ **1.** People can easily float on Great Salt Lake because

_____ **2.** Great Salt Lake has little animal life because

_____ **3.** Lake Bonneville shrank because

_____ **4.** The lake is saltier in some places than in others because

_____ **5.** The salts and minerals of the lake are valuable because

a. the water is too salty to support most animal life.

b. they are used in farming and industry.

c. the salty water is very buoyant.

d. the weather became hotter and drier.

e. a causeway separates the lake into two parts.

What Do You Think?
Discuss these questions.

1. Would you like to visit Great Salt Lake? Why or why not?

2. Bird-watching is popular with many people. Why do people enjoy this activity? Do you? Explain.

A Last Look
Write about one of these topics.

1. Because the old lake bed of Lake Bonneville is flat, it is a great place for racing cars. Learn more about the history of racing on the Bonneville salt flats.

2. Learn more about the birds you might see at Great Salt Lake. Describe one kind and tell why it lives at the lake.

Utah

Wyoming

Thinking about the Picture

1. What do you know about grizzly bears?
2. Why do people want to see bears and other animals in the wild?

Yellowstone National Park

The first U.S. national park was Yellowstone National Park, established in 1872. Yellowstone covers more than 2 million acres in northwestern Wyoming. It has some of North America's strangest scenery. Only one or two miles beneath the surface are hot lava and liquid rock. Steam, smoke, and gases come out of the ground at 10,000 points in the park. There are pools of boiling water or hot, bubbling mud. Minerals in the water color the rocks bright orange or yellow.

Sometimes pressure deep in the earth sends boiling water and steam high into the air. That is a geyser. Yellowstone has many geysers. The most famous geyser is "Old Faithful." It erupts regularly about 18 or 19 times a day. Crowds of tourists gather when Old Faithful is due to erupt. Steam and water spout as high as 185 feet (56 meters) into the air.

Yellowstone has a great variety of scenery. It has lakes, canyons, meadows, and forests. There are many kinds of wildflowers and wildlife. Almost 300 species of birds live in the park, including eagles, pelicans, and herons. Many kinds of fish swim in its rivers and lakes. Larger animals in the park include includes moose, bears, wolves, cougars, coyotes, and deer. There is a herd of 2,400 bison. In summer, thousands of elk roam the park.

Before 1895, fewer than 5,000 people a year visited Yellowstone. About 2.5 million people now visit annually. Park rangers work to keep Yellowstone safe for both tourists and wildlife.

The first white person to see Yellowstone was probably John Colter, in 1807. People didn't believe him. In the 1860s and 1870s, expeditions explored the West. They sent back photographs and drawings. That convinced both Congress and the public. In 1872, President Ulysses S. Grant signed a bill creating the park. That set the pattern for the U.S. National Park System.

Wyoming

A First Look at Vocabulary

Choose the best definition for each word in bold type.

_____ 1. **Pressure** builds within the earth until suddenly the geyser erupts.

         a. balance   b. force created by pushing   c. lightness of air

_____ 2. Most **geysers** do not erupt as regularly as Old Faithful does.

         a. spring that shoots up   b. lake of hot water   c. steam from pool

_____ 3. When the geyser **erupts,** it shoots water a hundred feet into the air.

         a. boils over   b. steams   c. shoots upward

_____ 4. Is the geyser **due** to erupt any time soon?

         a. late   b. needed   c. expected

_____ 5. Both **species** of North American bears live in the park.

         a. kinds   b. colors   c. sizes

_____ 6. Some people drive to Yellowstone **annually** to see the animals.

         a. every second year   b. only once   c. every year

_____ 7. John Colter first went west with the Lewis and Clark **expedition.**

         a. trip to explore   b. horseback ride   c. boat trip

_____ 8. Who **convinced** Congress that Yellowstone should be protected?

         a. sold   b. caused to agree   c. argued against

A Second Look at Vocabulary

Complete the sentences. Use the words from the first exercise.

1. Are you _____ that Yellowstone is a great place to visit?

2. When a geyser _____, it's not a good idea to stand too close.

3. Park rangers can tell you when Old Faithful is _____ to erupt.

4. Many _____ of animals live in the park.

5. Beneath the ground, the _____ keeps building until the steam rushes out.

6. Some of Yellowstone's _____ shoot water more than 200 feet high.

7. The people in the first _____ to reach Yellowstone must have been amazed.

8. Some birds migrate _____ each winter and return in the spring.

Wyoming

Understanding the Reading

Choose the best answer.

_____ 1. Yellowstone National Park
   a. is the only U.S. national park.
   b. was the first U.S. national park.
   c. has the world's only geysers.

_____ 2. Old Faithful
   a. is the highest geyser.
   b. is Yellowstone's only geyser.
   c. erupts regularly about 18 or 19 times a day.

_____ 3. Park rangers work hard to
   a. help keep tourists and wildlife both safe in the park.
   b. keep animals from getting in the way of people.
   c. keep too many people from coming into the park.

_____ 4. When John Colter told people about Yellowstone,
   a. Congress immediately made it a national park.
   b. people did not believe him at first.
   c. President Grant asked him to establish the park.

Fact or Opinion?

Mark each statement _F_ for _fact_ or _O_ for _opinion_.

_____ 1. Yellowstone is America's most interesting park.

_____ 2. Yellowstone is a safe place for wildlife.

_____ 3. President Grant and Congress acted wisely in creating Yellowstone National Park.

When Did It Happen?

Write numbers to put the events in the order they happened.

_____ 2.5 million people visited the park in a year.

_____ Expeditions visited Yellowstone.

_____ John Colter saw Yellowstone.

_____ Yellowstone was made a national park.

What Do You Think?
Discuss these questions.

1. Would you like to go to Yellowstone? Why or why not? If you went, what would you want to see first?

2. Do you think national parks are a good idea? Explain.

3. Grizzly bears are dangerous animals, and yet they roam free in the park. Is this a good idea? Explain.

A Last Look
Write about one of these topics.

1. Is the main purpose of a national park to protect animals and plants? Or is its main purpose to help people enjoy nature? Can too many people visit a park?

2. What is another national park in the United States? Compare and contrast it with Yellowstone.

Wyoming

Southwest Region

Arizona, New Mexico, Oklahoma, Texas

A Quick Look at this Region

The hot desert sun bakes the Southwest region. It is a land of mountains, deserts, and colorful canyons. Visitors are amazed by the rock formations carved by wind and water. The Grand Canyon is one of the world's natural wonders.

Native Americans have lived in the region for thousands of years. Navajo, Hopi, and Pueblo peoples have all contributed to Southwestern culture. In the 1500s, Spanish explorers took control of the region. In 1821, Mexico gained independence from Spain. This territory became Mexico. After the Mexican-American War in 1848, the land passed to the United States.

Water is crucial in this dry region. In the 1900s, several dams were built on large rivers. They supply water for irrigation. Farmers grow crops such as cotton, alfalfa, and citrus fruits. Cattle and sheep ranching is also important.

Natural gas and oil have brought wealth to the area, especially in Texas and Oklahoma. Other regional industries are computers, electronics, and aeronautics. New Mexico has been a center for nuclear research since World War II.

Arizona

Thinking about the Picture

1. What kind of place is the Grand Canyon? Describe the land. What kind of plants do you see?
2. Why do people want to visit places like this?

The Grand Canyon

The Grand Canyon in northwestern Arizona is one of Earth's natural wonders. If you stand at the rim of the canyon, the Colorado River is about a mile below you. The canyon is 277 river miles long. It varies between 1 mile and 18 miles wide.

It is hard to imagine that this small river carved this great canyon. In fact, it probably did only part of the job. Geologists do not agree on how or when the Grand Canyon was formed. One idea is that about 6 million years ago, a great upheaval raised the Rocky Mountains. The Colorado River began to rush downhill, carving through the rock. For several million years, the river cut the canyon deeper. Wind, rain, frost, and ice also wore away the rock walls, making it wider. Even now the canyon is changing.

The steep walls of the canyon display 13 colorful layers of rock. They show two billion years of Earth history. Many are brilliantly colored. At sunset, the red rocks seem to glow. The rocks are filled with fossils of ancient plants and animals. There are both sea plants and land animals. They are evidence that seas once covered this region.

Native Americans have lived in the canyon for about 4,000 years. In 1540, a Spanish explorer, Don Lopez de Cardenas, was the first European to see it. For centuries, the canyon remained fairly unknown. In 1869, John Wesley Powell, a scientist and soldier, explored it with a few men. He named it "Grand Canyon." In 1903, President Theodore Roosevelt made his first visit. He said, "Keep it for your children and your children's children, . . . as the one great sight which every American should see."

Grand Canyon National Park was opened in 1919. About 5 million people visit the park each year. Some drive around the canyon rim. Others ride on mules or hike down steep paths. Adventurous tourists can travel the river on whitewater rafts. It is a trip they will never forget.

Arizona

A First Look at Vocabulary

Match the words and phrases with their meanings.

_____ **1.** adventurous   a. part of ancient animal or plant preserved in rock

_____ **2.** canyon   b. rapidly moving water with bubbles or foam

_____ **3.** evidence   c. proof

_____ **4.** fossil   d. edge

_____ **5.** layers   e. flat boat

_____ **6.** raft   f. rising or falling sharply

_____ **7.** rim   g. upward movement

_____ **8.** steep   h. parts or levels, one on top of another

_____ **9.** upheaval   i. narrow valley with high cliffs

_____ **10.** whitewater   j. willing to take risks

A Second Look at Vocabulary

Complete the story. Use the words from the first exercise.

Millions of people visit the Grand Canyon each year. Most stay on the

_____ where they can look down into the _____ at
     1   2

the river a mile below. The walls of the canyon are _____. They seem
                                            3

to go straight down. The walls are also colorful. You can see _____ of
                                            4

rock. Each is a different color. An ancient _____ of the land has raised
                                            5

the rim of the Grand Canyon to about seven thousand feet above sea level.

Some people choose to walk into the canyon. Many of the trails are only a few feet wide.

Hikers must be _____ to risk these trails. As they walk, hikers might see
                                    6

_____ of the ancient sea that covered the land. They might even find a
     7

_____ of an animal that lived millions of years ago.
     8

The Colorado River can be violent. As it pours over rocks it becomes _____.
                                            9

A fearless person might float down the river on a _____.
                              10

Understanding the Reading

Choose the best answer.

_____ **1.** The Grand Canyon
   a. has formed over the past million years.
   b. is about a mile deep.
   c. is closed to visitors.

_____ **2.** The walls of the Grand Canyon
   a. light up brilliantly at sunset.
   b. are about one-half mile apart.
   c. are too steep for people walk down them to the river.

_____ **3.** The Grand Canyon was named by
   a. Don Lopez de Cardenas.
   b. John Wesley Powell.
   c. President Theodore Roosevelt.

Reading between the Lines

Look carefully at the reading. Mark each statement _T_ for _true_ or _F_ for _false_.

_____ **1.** Native Americans never lived in the Grand Canyon.

_____ **2.** Tourists can ride in buses down into the canyon.

_____ **3.** President Roosevelt explored the Grand Canyon.

Why Did It Happen?

Match the sentence parts.

_____ **1.** The Grand Canyon was carved by

_____ **2.** The Grand Canyon was made wider by

_____ **3.** Fossils show that

_____ **4.** The area got much higher because

   a. an ancient sea once covered the area.

   b. an upheaval pushed the land upward.

   c. wind, rain, frost, and ice.

   d. the Colorado River.

What Do You Think?

Discuss these questions.

1. What do you think Don Lopez de Cardenas thought when he first saw the Grand Canyon? Do you think today's visitors feel the same way?

2. How would you like to see the Grand Canyon? By car, foot, mule, or raft? Explain.

A Last Look

Write about one of these topics.

1. Why do you think President Roosevelt thought every American should see the Grand Canyon? Do you agree with him? Why or why not?

2. Learn about a mule ride to the bottom of the Grand Canyon or a raft trip down the river. Describe what a visitor would do and see on the trip.

3. The Grand Canyon is more than one mile deep. Is the weather different on the rim than it is on the canyon floor? Write a comparison of the weather in the two places.

Arizona

New Mexico

Thinking about the Pictures

1. Describe the clothing these people are wearing. How are they like the clothes you wear? How are they different?
2. What are these people making? Do you use these items?

The Pueblo

Several groups of Native Americans live in New Mexico. They make up about 9.5 percent of the state's population. The Pueblo, Navajo, Zuni, and Apache have different cultures.

By about AD 100, the ancestors of today's Pueblo were living in the "Four Corners." That is the place where New Mexico, Arizona, Utah, and Colorado meet. Their neighbors called them "Anasazi." The Anasazi built houses many stories high on the sides of steep cliffs. These protected them from other tribes. From about 700 to 1050, they had one of the most advanced civilizations in North America. They made cotton cloth, pottery, and baskets. They grew turkeys, squash, corn, and beans. Then, for some reason, they moved away.

Spanish explorers arrived here in 1540. The Anasazi's descendants were living in villages. The Spanish called them "pueblos," which means "towns" in Spanish. The Spanish made the Pueblo people work for them. They tried to wipe out the traditional Pueblo way of life. The Pueblo, however, secretly kept their traditional dances and ceremonies.

In 1680, the Pueblo leader Popé led a rebellion against the Spanish. For a short time, the Pueblo were free of Spanish rule. However, they were often at war with the Navajo and Apache. In 1692, the Spanish took control again. When Mexico became independent in 1821, it included this area. At the end of the Mexican-American War in 1848, the United States took over.

Today most Pueblo live in 19 villages, also called pueblos. Most are along the Rio Grande River in New Mexico and Arizona. Pueblo peoples speak six different languages. Like their ancestors, they build houses of adobe—dried clay or mud. Pueblo artists make and sell traditional jewelry, pottery, and baskets. Each pueblo has its own pottery design. For years, the Pueblo fought to keep their culture. Now they can proudly teach their traditions.

A First Look at Vocabulary

Choose the best definition for each word in bold type.

_____ 1. The culture of the Pueblo people was very **advanced.**
   a. simple   b. highly developed   c. old

_____ 2. The Pueblo **civilization** goes back to the 700s.
   a. rebellion   b. houses   c. culture

_____ 3. Pueblo people make beautiful **pottery.**
   a. clothing   b. knives and forks   c. dishes and bowls

_____ 4. The **ancestors** of the Pueblo people were living there for centuries.
   a. children   b. enemies   c. relatives from the past

_____ 5. Did the Pueblo people **convert** to the Roman Catholic religion?
   a. begin   b. change   c. compare

_____ 6. The Pueblo people are not **independent** of the federal government.
   a. different   b. connected to   c. free

_____ 7. The walls of the house are made from **adobe.**
   a. dried mud   b. wood   c. mud and wood

_____ 8. Some Pueblo people make very beautiful **jewelry.**
   a. tools   b. rings and necklaces   c. traditional clothing

A Second Look at Vocabulary

Complete the sentences. Use the words from the first exercise.

1. The Pueblo were _____ for only 12 years before the Spanish took over again.

2. People still build houses out of _____ today.

3. This ancient _____ built large cities.

4. As the Pueblo became more _____, they made better pottery.

5. Do you have Native American rings or other _____?

6. They used the _____ to carry water and to cook in.

7. No one is sure what happened to the _____ of the Pueblo.

Understanding the Reading

Choose the best answer.

_____ 1. The ancestors of today's Pueblo were the
   a. Zuni.
   b. Navajo.
   c. Anasazi.

_____ 2. When the Spanish came, they
   a. tried to wipe out the Pueblo way of life.
   b. tried to learn about Anasazi culture.
   c. could not find evidence of the Anasazi.

_____ 3. Most Pueblo now live in
   a. large cities far from their homeland.
   b. pueblos near the Rio Grande River in New Mexico and Arizona.
   c. ordinary houses in cities in New Mexico and Arizona.

Fact or Opinion?

Mark each statement _F_ for _fact_ or _O_ for _opinion_.

_____ 1. The Anasazi had the most advanced civilization in North America.

_____ 2. The Spanish wanted the Pueblo to be more like Europeans.

_____ 3. The Pueblo want to continue their traditions.

_____ 4. Pueblo are the most important group in New Mexico.

Where's the Idea?

These are main ideas from the reading. Write the number of the paragraph where you find each idea.

_____ The Pueblo lands have been controlled by several nations.

_____ Several groups of Native Americans live in New Mexico.

_____ The Anasazi had an advanced civilization.

_____ The Pueblo now can follow their own culture.

_____ Spanish explorers took control of Pueblo villages in 1540.

What Do You Think?

Discuss these questions.

1. Why do you think the Spanish wanted to wipe out traditional Pueblo culture? Why did the Pueblo want to continue their traditions?

2. Would you want to live the traditional lifestyle of the Pueblo? Explain.

A Last Look

Write about one of these topics.

1. Learn about one of the Anasazi cultural areas that is now protected. These include Chaco Culture National Historic Park, Bandelier National Monument, El Morro National Monument, and Aztec Ruins National Monument. Describe what can be seen at the site.

2. Find out about one of the traditional Pueblo arts, such as jewelry, pottery, or baskets. What makes the art special? What materials are used? What traditional symbols are used in decorating the art?

Oklahoma

Thinking about the Picture

1. What do you think these Native Americans are doing? How do you know?
2. How were Native Americans treated in U.S. history?

The Trail of Tears

 Oklahoma ranks second among the states in the number of Native Americans who live there. In the 2000 census, more than 273,000 people in the state said they were Native American. About 118,000 others have Native American ancestors. Those ancestors, though, probably did not live in Oklahoma. The U.S. government sent them there.

European settlers came to the southeast United States in the 1600s. Five major Indian nations lived there. They were the Cherokee, Choctaw, Chickasaw, Creek, and Seminole. They lived in towns and farmed the land. So settlers called them the Five Civilized Tribes.

As more settlers arrived, they wanted the Indian lands. One by one, Native American peoples were forced to move to poor land farther west. In 1829, gold was found on Cherokee land in Georgia. That increased pressure. In 1830, Congress passed the Indian Removal Act. It ordered all Native Americans to move west of the Mississippi River. The government told the Five Civilized Tribes to move to Oklahoma, then called "Indian Territory." But the five nations resisted. The president sent in the U.S. Army.

During the 1830s, soldiers forced the tribes off their lands. The Choctaw went first, in 1831, then the Creek and the Chickasaw. Thousands died of hunger, cold, or disease.

The Cherokee resisted stubbornly. In 1838, soldiers rounded up as many as 17,000 Cherokee and forced them into camps. A few escaped and stayed behind in the Smoky Mountains. Over the winter, the rest were moved to Oklahoma. They went by foot, on horseback, or in wagons. Thousands died on the way. History books call this journey "The Trail of Tears."

In Florida, the Seminole also fought back. They lost their war, and most left for the West in 1842. All five nations set up their own governments in Oklahoma.

Oklahoma

A First Look at Vocabulary

Choose the best definition for each word in bold type.

_____ 1. The **census** shows that almost 300,000 Native Americans live in Oklahoma.
   a. population   b. government   c. official count

_____ 2. The Cherokee were one of the **civilized** tribes.
   a. living by farming   b. having a high social organization   c. living by hunting

_____ 3. The winter cold **increased** the risk of illness.
   a. stopped the need   b. made less   c. made greater

_____ 4. Congress **passed** a bill that forced the tribes to move.
   a. approved   b. talked about   c. voted on

_____ 5. The army **ordered** the Creek to move.
   a. asked   b. suggested   c. told

_____ 6. Which tribes **resisted** the army when they were told to move west?
   a. looked for   b. fought against   c. agreed with

_____ 7. The army **rounded up** all the people and led them to Oklahoma.
   a. made them stand   b. gathered together   c. made them walk

_____ 8. The people who **escaped** stayed behind in the east.
   a. got away   b. joined   c. arrived late

A Second Look at Vocabulary

Complete the sentences. Use the words from the first exercise.

1. Congress _____ the bill, and then the army went to make the tribes move.

2. The people _____ their horses and cattle and began the long walk.

3. The president _____ the army to take the Choctaw to Oklahoma.

4. They were called _____ because they were peaceful and lived in towns.

5. Every 10 years, we have a _____ to count the people in the U.S.

6. Interest in the land _____ because gold was found.

7. How many of the Cherokee _____ from the army and stayed in the east?

8. The five nations _____ the army, but the army was too strong.

Oklahoma

145

Understanding the Reading

Choose the best answer.

_____ 1. Settlers called the five tribes the civilized tribes because
   a. they lived in towns and farmed.
   b. they spoke English.
   c. they did not fight the settlers.

_____ 2. The five tribes were moved because
   a. they were at war with the U.S. government.
   b. they wanted better land in Oklahoma.
   c. the settlers wanted their land.

_____ 3. The long trip to Oklahoma by the Cherokees is called the
   a. longest journey in American history.
   b. Trail of Tears.
   c. Indian Removal Act.

Reading between the Lines

Look carefully at the reading. Mark each statement _T_ for _true_ or _F_ for _false_.

_____ 1. Very few Native Americans live in Oklahoma today.

_____ 2. The five tribes refused to move because they wanted gold.

_____ 3. The Seminole were the last of the five tribes to go to Oklahoma.

_____ 4. The army gave the people plenty of food during the journey to Oklahoma.

When Did It Happen?

Write numbers to put the events in the order they happened.

_____ Gold was discovered in Cherokee land in Georgia.

_____ The Cherokee were moved to Oklahoma.

_____ The five tribes moved into towns and began farming.

_____ The Choctaw were moved to Oklahoma.

_____ Congress passed the Indian Removal Act.

What Do You Think?
Discuss these questions.

1. In the 1800s, Native Americans were moved off of land they had lived on for hundreds of years. Could people be treated like this today? Explain.

2. Should the U.S. government make up for the unfair treatment of Native Americans in the past? Explain.

A Last Look
Write about one of these topics.

1. Choose one of the five tribes. Where does the tribe live today? How many people are in the tribe? Have they kept their culture? How?

2. Who was Sequoyah? Why was he important in Cherokee history?

Oklahoma

Texas

Thinking about the Picture

1. What is this man doing? What tools is he using? What animals do you see?
2. Do you think this work is difficult? Why or why not?

Cowboys

The Age of the Cowboy began after the Civil War. In 1865, Texas was the open range, with no fences. About six million cattle wandered over the grasslands. So ranch owners hired cowboys to round up cattle on the range. Then they herded them over the long trails to Missouri, Kansas, and Nebraska. From there, trains took the cattle to eastern stockyards, where they sold for high prices.

Most people's ideas about cowboys come from the movies. Hollywood cowboys were always white. They spoke English. Real cowboys were quite different. Some were ex-soldiers who had fought in the Civil War. Others were young men from the East, looking for adventure. Many were not white. About one fourth were Mexican. Another one fourth were black Americans. Others were Native Americans. A few were women. Many cowboys spoke Spanish.

Mexican cowboys were called "vaqueros." A cowboy's typical clothing copied the practical work clothes of a vaquero. The big cowboy hat imitated his "sombrero." Vaqueros also wore leather trousers, or "chaps." Cowboys also learned to use a rope, or "lasso," to catch and tie up cattle.

Cowboys were usually young. The work was difficult, dangerous, and lonely. The pay was low. They worked long hours. Every spring and fall they rounded up cattle. They branded newborn calves with the ranch's symbol. Most important, they drove huge herds for hundreds of miles to the railroads.

In the terrible winter of 1886 to 1887, hundreds of thousands of cattle died. After that, many cowboys settled down on farms. Farmers closed off the open range with fences. The railroads reached Texas. The Age of the Cowboy had lasted only 20 years.

Modern cowboys still take care of cattle. Today, though, they move them by truck and use helicopters to find strays.

A First Look at Vocabulary

Match each term with its meaning.

_____ **1.** range   a. usual

_____ **2.** wandered   b. long, thick cord

_____ **3.** westward   c. open grassland where cattle feed

_____ **4.** herded   d. burned with a symbol

_____ **5.** stockyard   e. animals that have wandered off

_____ **6.** typical   f. guided animals in a group

_____ **7.** imitated   g. fenced area where animals are kept

_____ **8.** rope   h. toward the west

_____ **9.** branded   i. traveled around without a plan

_____ **10.** strays   j. copied

A Second Look at Vocabulary

Complete the sentences. Use the words from the first exercise.

1. Many people have _____ cowboys by dressing in cowboy clothes.

2. The _____ cowboy still wears a cowboy hat and boots.

3. The cattle were kept in a _____ until the trains came.

4. Cowboys rode long distances to find _____ that got separated from the herds.

5. The cattle roamed freely over the _____.

6. Many settlers traveled _____ to find land of their own.

7. They _____ cattle so the owners would know which ones belonged to them.

8. The cowboy threw a _____ over the head of the cow.

9. Cattle _____ across the land eating grass and drinking from the streams.

10. The cowboys _____ the cattle into large groups.

Understanding the Reading

Choose the best answer.

_____ 1. Why did cowboys herd cattle to Missouri, Kansas, and Nebraska?
   a. The railroads had reached those states.
   b. The cattle sold for high prices in those states.
   c. The cattle had wandered far from Texas.

_____ 2. Why don't most people know much about real cowboys?
   a. There have never been real cowboys.
   b. People get their ideas about cowboys from watching movies.
   c. Very little is known about cowboys in the 1800s.

_____ 3. Why did cowboys imitate the Mexican vaqueros?
   a. The vaqueros sold boots and hats cheaply.
   b. Cowboys thought the vaqueros were heroes.
   c. The vaqueros had taken care of cattle in Texas for a long time.

_____ 4. Why did the age of the cowboy end?
   a. Many cattle died, farmers fenced off the open range, and railroads reached Texas.
   b. The Civil War started and the cowboys went to fight in the war.
   c. Cattle could no longer be sold for high prices in the east.

Where's the Idea?

There are main ideas from the reading. Write the number of the paragraph where you find each idea.

_____ Real cowboys came from many different groups.

_____ Modern cowboys still care for cattle, but their tools have changed.

_____ The age of the cowboy ended in about 1887.

_____ Cowboys wore clothing like that of the Mexican vaqueros.

_____ Railroads had not reached Texas, so cowboys herded the cattle to Missouri, Kansas, and Nebraska.

_____ Cowboys worked hard.

What Do You Think?
Discuss these questions.

1. Do you like movies about cowboys? Why or why not?

2. Why don't movies show what cowboys were really like?

3. Would you like to be a cowboy today? Why or why not?

A Last Look
Write about one of these topics.

1. Learn about a Texas "cattle drive"—the long trip when cowboys herded the cattle north. What did a cowboy do? How long did the trip take? What were the dangers on the trip?

2. Cowboys cared for longhorn cattle. Learn about these cattle. How were they different from today's cattle?

Pacific Coast Region

Alaska, California, Hawaii, Oregon, Washington

A Quick Look at this Region

The states in the Pacific Ocean region face west toward Asia. Trade with other nations in the Pacific, such as Japan, is important. In the Pacific Northwest, the weather is mild and rainy. The California climate is drier. Mountain ranges run the length of the Pacific Coast.

Washington and Oregon are centers for high-tech industry. Many people work in computers and aerospace. California is America's richest and most populous state. It ranks first in the nation in sales of farm products. Many Californians work in tourism and the entertainment industry.

Alaska and Hawaii became the 49th and 50th states in 1959. The tropical islands of Hawaii are 2,400 miles southwest of the mainland. Polynesians first settled the islands about 1,500 years ago. The United States took possession of Hawaii in 1898. American businesses introduced the growing of pineapples and sugar. Hawaii's weather and scenery attract many tourists.

By contrast, part of Alaska is in the Arctic. Summers are cool, winters very cold. Alaska is the largest state in land area, but its population is small. It has rich resources, including oil and gold.

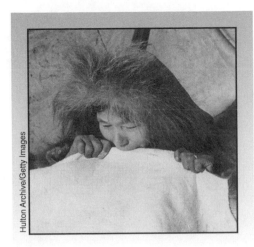

Alaska

Thinking about the Picture

1. This woman is crimping the skin to soften the hide. What do you think she will do with this skin when she is finished?
2. What does this activity tell you about her culture?

The Inuit

 Nearly 16 percent of the people in Alaska identify themselves as Alaska Natives or Native Americans. The largest group—more than 40,000—are Inuit. In their language, *Inuit* means "the people." They are sometimes called Eskimos, but they prefer the name *Inuit*. Other Inuit live in Canada, Greenland, and Russia.

The Inuit and other native peoples came from northeast Asia. About 5,000 years ago, they began to move into Alaska, searching for food. The weather here is often bitterly cold. To survive, the Inuit lived and hunted in groups. Near the sea, they caught fish, whales, seals, and walrus. They also hunted polar bears, foxes, Arctic hare, and caribou, a kind of deer.

Animals were useful in other ways. Teams of dogs pulled their sleds across the snow. Out of animal skins, the Inuit made warm clothes and tents. They built small, waterproof skin boats called kayaks. Out of the teeth, bones, and antlers of animals, they made tools and weapons for hunting. They also carved pins and buttons showing seals, fish, and other animals.

The Inuit way of life began to change when Europeans came to Alaska in the 1600s. The first European settlers were Russian traders. They hunted and traded animal skins. In 1867, Russia sold Alaska to the United States.

Today, most Inuit no longer live in traditional houses or wear traditional clothes. They use snowmobiles instead of dog teams. They use up-to-date tools. Some, however, continue to hunt and fish for a living.

Other Inuit follow traditional ways. They live in small villages and speak their native languages. During the long, cold winters, they live in houses built of snow or earth and stone. In the short, cool summers, they live in animal-skin tents. Today, there is a new interest in Inuit culture, language, and art. Many Inuit want to keep these alive for future generations.

A First Look at Vocabulary

Match each term with its meaning.

_____ **1.** identify   a. vehicle without a motor that travels on snow

_____ **2.** prefer   b. type of boat

_____ **3.** bitterly   c. name (a person or thing)

_____ **4.** survive   d. small motor vehicle with skis that travels on snow

_____ **5.** sled   e. sharply or cuttingly

_____ **6.** kayak   f. easily carried

_____ **7.** weapon   g. continue to live

_____ **8.** snowmobile   h. like better

_____ **9.** portable   i. tool for killing

A Second Look at Vocabulary

Choose the best answer to complete each sentence.

_____ **1.** In the far north, summers are cool and winters are ____ cold.
   a. mildly   b. traditionally   c. bitterly

_____ **2.** Many of the Alaska people ____ themselves as Inuit.
   a. identify   b. choose   c. prefer

_____ **3.** An Inuit travels long distances across the sea in a ____.
   a. snowmobile   b. kayak   c. sled

_____ **4.** The tents are ____, so they can be easily moved from place to place.
   a. heavy   b. native   c. portable

_____ **5.** The ____ that most Inuit use for hunting is the gun.
   a. weapon   b. antler   c. pins

_____ **6.** The Inuit ____ in one of the most dangerous places on earth.
   a. search   b. survive   c. carve

_____ **7.** Hunters travel faster across the snow on a ____ than on a sled.
   a. kayak   b. snowmobile   c. team

_____ **8.** Do they ____ to be called Inuit or Eskimos?
   a. search   b. identify   c. prefer

_____ **9.** They carry things in a ____ that is pulled over the snow by dogs.
   a. sled   b. car   c. snowmobile

Alaska

Understanding the Reading

Choose the best answer.

_____ **1.** The Inuit and other Native people
   a. make up more than one-half of the population of Alaska.
   b. came to Alaska from northeast Asia.
   c. came to Alaska with the Europeans during the 1600s.

_____ **2.** In the past, the Inuit survived by
   a. hunting and fishing.
   b. trading with the Europeans and Russians.
   c. farming.

_____ **3.** The Inuit
   a. used animal skins to make clothes, tents, and kayaks.
   b. stayed away from dangerous animals like polar bears.
   c. ate few fish because the sea was frozen most of the year.

_____ **4.** The Inuit way of life
   a. remains much the same today as it was long ago.
   b. began to change when the Europeans arrived.
   c. is being lost because people are no longer interested in the traditional ways of life.

_____ **5.** Inuit who live in traditional ways
   a. live in tents in the summer and houses in the winter.
   b. have left Alaska and returned to Russia, Canada, and Greenland.
   c. use snowmobiles to hunt for polar bears and caribou.

Reading between the Lines

Look carefully at the reading. Mark each statement _T_ for _true_ or _F_ for _false_.

_____ **1.** All of Alaska's native people are called Inuit.

_____ **2.** All the Inuit live in Alaska.

_____ **3.** To survive, the Inuit used many parts of the animals.

_____ **4.** The native languages of the Inuit have been forgotten.

_____ **5.** Most Inuit still follow a traditional way of life today.

What Do You Think?
Discuss these questions.

1. What problems might Inuit have in changing from their traditional way of life to a modern way of life?

2. What problems might the Inuit have in trying to continue living a traditional way of life? Do you think older or younger people will have more problems living a traditional life? Why?

A Last Look
Write about one of these topics.

1. Read about the sale of Alaska to the United States. Then write a summary of the main events.

2. During the winter, some Inuit live in houses built of snow, called igloos. Learn about these houses. How are they built? What are they like? Why are they a good winter home for this region?

California

Thinking about the Picture

1. What does this sign make you think about?

2. What do you know about the history of movies?

3. Why do you think people like movies so much?

The Movie Industry

The big white letters on a hill in Los Angeles say "Hollywood." That famous sign makes people think about movies. In the early 1900s, this part of California became the center of a new industry—motion pictures.

In the United States, motion pictures were first made in the 1890s in New York and New Jersey. But the year-round sunny weather in California made it a better place for filming. There were other reasons, too. At the time, land in California was cheaper. Taxes were lower. The variety of natural scenery around Los Angeles was ideal for filming.

D.W. Griffith was Hollywood's first great director. He made hundreds of short silent films between 1908 and 1913. He next made several major films, such as *Intolerance* (1916). Griffith introduced new ideas, such as close-up shots. He also discovered new stars. Some early stars were Douglas Fairbanks, Mary Pickford, and Charlie Chaplin.

A number of European immigrants came to Los Angeles. They built movie studios in nearby Hollywood. By the 1930s, there were five large studios there. Today, only Paramount Studio is left in Hollywood itself. However, there are studios in other parts of Los Angeles and in cities around it. Making movies is still a major business in southern California.

Hollywood has many reminders of the movies. Stars on the Walk of Fame honor favorite entertainers. Stone and bronze stars are placed in the sidewalks, each with a performer's name written on it. Another tradition began in 1927, when a movie star left her footprints in wet cement in front of Grauman's (now Mann's) Chinese Theatre. Many other stars have left their prints there.

Besides these Hollywood sights, tourists can visit studios to see how movies are made. They can also watch the filming of TV shows.

A First Look at Vocabulary

Choose the best definition for each word in bold type.

_____ 1. The weather in Hollywood is pleasant **year-round.**
   a. once a year   b. this year   c. all year

_____ 2. California's mountains and beaches are **ideal** for many movies.
   a. perfect   b. good   c. bad

_____ 3. The **director** wanted the actor to show more anger.
   a. person in charge of a film   b. person who watches a film   c. person who acts in a film

_____ 4. One of the first important **films** was _Intolerance._
   a. plays   b. shows   c. movies

_____ 5. The director asked for a **shot** of the clouds over the ocean.
   a. reminder   b. picture   c. movement

_____ 6. The **studio** was busy as people got ready to make the new film.
   a. where films are seen   b. where people wait   c. where films are made

_____ 7. The **entertainer** was happy to work on the film.
   a. person in charge of a film   b. actor, dancer, or musician   c. worker

_____ 8. You can see the footprint of a famous actor in the **cement.**
   a. type of hard surface   b. top of a table   c. type of picture

A Second Look at Vocabulary

Complete the sentences. Use the words from the first exercise.

1. The _____ actor should be tall and handsome.

2. The director wanted an _____ who could sing as well as act.

3. Movie stars are invited to place their footprints in the _____.

4. A _____ must choose the actors and tell them what to do.

5. The director and actors come to the _____ early each day to start work.

6. The _____ made in California are watched around the world.

7. Films are made _____ at studios in California.

8. Sometimes the _____ should be a close-up of an actor's face.

Understanding the Reading

Choose the best answer.

_____ 1. Hollywood became the center of the movie industry
because
a. D.W. Griffith lived in Hollywood.
b. Los Angeles had sunshine, cheap land, and low taxes.
c. many of the early stars lived there.

_____ 2. Today, large movie studios
a. remain in or near Los Angeles.
b. are all in Hollywood.
c. have all moved to cities outside California.

_____ 3. The Walk of Fame has
a. footprints of famous stars.
b. stone and bronze stars with actors' names.
c. movies, costumes, and other reminders of great movies.

Fact or Opinion?

Mark each statement *F* for *fact* or *O* for *opinion*.

_____ 1. Films were first made in New York and New Jersey.

_____ 2. D.W. Griffith introduced many new ideas to filming.

_____ 3. The best early stars were Douglas Fairbanks, Mary
Pickford, and Charlie Chaplin.

_____ 4. The world's best movies are still made in Los Angeles.

When Did It Happen?

Write numbers to put the events in the order they happened.

_____ D.W. Griffith made hundreds of short films.

_____ The first motion pictures were made.

_____ Five large motion picture studios were built in Hollywood.

_____ The first footprints were left on the sidewalk in front of
Grauman's Chinese Theatre.

What Do You Think?
Discuss these questions.

1. Who is your favorite film
star? Why?
2. What is your favorite
movie? Why?
3. Would you like to visit
Hollywood? Why?

A Last Look
Write about one of these
topics.

1. Learn about one of your
favorite movies. Where
was it filmed? Why?
2. How did movies change
when sound was added?
Did movies become more
popular? Were the same
stars successful in the new
movies?

Hawaii

Thinking about the Picture

1. This is an Hawaiian green turtle. Have you seen animals like it before? Where?
2. How would you feel if animals like this one died out?

Rare Plants and Animals

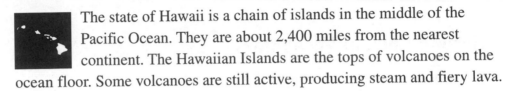

The state of Hawaii is a chain of islands in the middle of the Pacific Ocean. They are about 2,400 miles from the nearest continent. The Hawaiian Islands are the tops of volcanoes on the ocean floor. Some volcanoes are still active, producing steam and fiery lava.

Because of its history and location, Hawaii has many rare plants and animals. When the islands were first formed, nothing lived there. Over millions of years, the volcanic rock cooled, and soil formed. Winds and birds carried seeds to the islands. The seeds sprouted and grew. In the new conditions, the plants changed. They grew into varieties that exist nowhere else on earth.

Some of Hawaii's unusual plants still grow today. One is the silversword, which grows in the mountains. It blooms once after about 25 years, then dies.

Before people came to Hawaii, the only mammals were bats and seals. There were hundreds of kinds of birds, many unique to Hawaii. There were thousands of species of insects. There were no amphibians or reptiles, except green turtles. According to the National Park Service, Hawaii's 10,000 native species of plants and animals developed from about 2,000 ancestor species.

The arrival of humans was a disaster for native plants and animals. The first settlers were the Polynesians, who arrived about AD 500. They became the native Hawaiians. But they brought dogs, pigs, chickens, and rats. Because they needed food, the Polynesians killed many birds. The British arrived in 1778. They brought other animals, as well as new fruits and vegetables. These drove out many native species.

Today, many of Hawaii's plants and animals are in danger of disappearing. More than 85 native birds are extinct. Many more are endangered. Even Hawaii's state bird, a goose called the nene, is endangered. Special programs now protect monk seals and other creatures.

Hawaii

A First Look at Vocabulary

Match each term with its meaning.

_____ **1.** island

_____ **2.** continent

_____ **3.** volcano

_____ **4.** rare

_____ **5.** sprouted

_____ **6.** thorn

_____ **7.** extinct

_____ **8.** endangered

a. a short, sharp growth on a plant stem

b. began growing

c. small land area surrounded by water

d. at risk of becoming extinct

e. one of Earth's very large land areas

f. not often seen

g. mountain that throws out lava and steam

h. no longer living or existing

A Second Look at Vocabulary

Choose the best answer to complete each sentence.

_____ **1.** People travel long distances to see some of Hawaii's ____ animals.

    a. rare   b. common   c. usual

_____ **2.** Some of Hawaii's ____ are making steam and lava now.

    a. islands   b. volcanoes   c. mountains

_____ **3.** Hawaii has more than eight main ____.

    a. thorns   b. continents   c. islands

_____ **4.** Once a plant becomes ____, it is gone forever.

    a. endangered   b. extinct   c. rare

_____ **5.** A plant that is ____ might be saved if people protect it.

    a. endangered   b. extinct   c. disappeared

_____ **6.** A seed fell onto the soil and then ____ and grew tall.

    a. formed   b. sprouted   c. developed

_____ **7.** Hawaii is not part of the ____ of North America.

    a. continent   b. country   c. island

_____ **8.** A rose has ____ that help protect it from its enemies.

    a. thorns   b. leaves   c. roots

Hawaii

Understanding the Reading

Choose the best answer.

_____ **1.** The state of Hawaii is a chain of islands that
   a. was first discovered by Polynesians in about 1900.
   b. is close to the Pacific Coast of California.
   c. are the tops of volcanoes.

_____ **2.** Before people arrived in Hawaii, the islands had
   a. two mammals, hundreds of birds, and thousands of insects.
   b. almost no animal life of any kind.
   c. dogs, pigs, chickens, and rats.

_____ **3.** Many of Hawaii's native plants and animals
   a. are spreading to other parts of the world.
   b. are endangered or extinct.
   c. keep animals from other places from surviving on the islands.

Reading between the Lines

Look carefully at the reading. Mark each statement _T_ for _true_ or _F_ for _false_.

_____ **1.** Before people arrived, the only mammals were bats and seals.

_____ **2.** The first Polynesian settlers did not hurt the native Hawaiian species.

_____ **3.** Today, people are trying to save some native species.

When Did It Happen?

Write numbers to put the events in the order they happened.

_____ Winds and birds carried seeds to the islands.

_____ Hawaii was formed by volcanoes.

_____ The plants changed because of new conditions.

_____ Many native species were endangered by the new species.

_____ The seeds sprouted and grew.

_____ Plants and animals were brought to the islands by settlers.

What Do You Think?
Discuss these questions.

1. Why do some people worry about plants and animals becoming extinct? Do you agree with them? Why?

2. How can people help preserve endangered species? What can you do?

A Last Look
Write about one of these topics.

1. What are some plants or animals that are endangered in your state or area? What is being done to protect them?

2. How do dogs, pigs, and rats hurt Hawaii's native species? What can be done to help these species?

Hawaii

Oregon

Thinking about the Picture

1. What is this man doing?
2. What are trees used for? Where do we get all the trees we need?

The Timber Industry

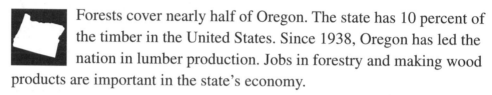 Forests cover nearly half of Oregon. The state has 10 percent of the timber in the United States. Since 1938, Oregon has led the nation in lumber production. Jobs in forestry and making wood products are important in the state's economy.

The Hudson's Bay Company began the timber industry here in 1827. By 1891, Oregon's timber industry was important for the region. Most of the forests belonged to the federal government. However, public lands were often not used wisely. In 1891, Congress set up forest reserves on federal lands. In 1907, forest reserves were renamed national forests.

Strict laws protected the national forests. For the next 50 years, logging was limited. But by the 1950s, there was little timber left for sale on private lands. Logging on federal lands increased. After World War II, there was a boom in building houses. As demand for wood increased, logging companies cut more trees in the national forests.

In the 1970s, new laws were passed to protect Oregon's wild areas. Some affected the logging industry. When trees are cut down, new trees must be planted. Some trees must be left uncut to provide habitat for birds and animals. That led to conflicts between environmentalists and the logging industry.

In 1990, the U.S. Fish and Wildlife Service said that the northern spotted owl was endangered. The old-growth forests where it lived were disappearing. To protect them, logging was limited in some areas. Some loggers lost jobs and blamed it on the law. Environmentalists argued that the living national forests were also an important resource. Changes in technology were already reducing the number of jobs in logging.

The timber industry is now in second place in Oregon's economy. High technology is in first place.

A First Look at Vocabulary

Choose the best definition for each word in bold type.

_____ 1. Oregon's **timber** provides lumber for building houses.

    a. industry   b. large trees   c. national forests

_____ 2. The trees are cut into **lumber** that is used for building.

    a. large trees   b. logs   c. flat pieces of wood

_____ 3. Why does Congress pass **strict** laws to control our national forests?

    a. new   b. national   c. requiring discipline

_____ 4. A **boom** in house building creates jobs for many people.

    a. rapid increase   b. loud noise   c. slow growth

_____ 5. The **demand** for timber increases during a boom in building.

    a. cost   b. need   c. hard work

_____ 6. Cutting old forests **affected** the ability of spotted owls to live.

    a. increased   b. decreased   c. influenced

_____ 7. Old-growth timber provides the right **habitat** for some animals.

    a. place to live   b. food   c. industry

_____ 8. People became angry during the **conflict** over protecting the forest.

    a. discussion   b. argument   c. economy

A Second Look at Vocabulary

Complete the sentences. Use the words from the first exercise.

1. Environmentalists believe the laws are not _____ enough to protect the forests.

2. A logger looks at the forest and sees jobs that cutting the _____ will create.

3. The _____ between loggers and environmentalists could not be avoided.

4. The logs are cut into pieces and then made into _____ for building houses.

5. Jobs in logging were _____ by cutting too many trees and not planting more.

6. When many people build houses, there is a _____ in jobs in the timber industry.

7. Cutting down the forests destroyed the _____ of many animals living there.

8. The _____ for lumber increases when people want new houses.

Understanding the Reading

Choose the best answer.

_____ 1. Oregon's timber industry
  a. no longer produces much lumber.
  b. was closed to protect the spotted owl.
  c. leads the country in the production of lumber.

_____ 2. Most of the forests of Oregon
  a. belong to the federal government.
  b. are closed to the timber industry.
  c. belong to the Hudson's Bay Company.

_____ 3. Laws passed in the 1970s
  a. protected some of Oregon's wild areas.
  b. ended the conflict between environmentalists and loggers.
  c. allowed loggers to cut more trees.

_____ 4. When logging in old-growth forests was limited during the 1990s, loggers
  a. began cutting more trees on the public lands.
  b. began cutting more trees on private lands.
  c. blamed the laws that protected the spotted owl.

_____ 5. Today, the timber industry
  a. is second to high technology in Oregon's economy.
  b. is Oregon's most important industry.
  c. cuts timber only from private forests.

Reading between the Lines

Look carefully at the reading. Mark each statement _T_ for _true_ or _F_ for _false_.

_____ 1. The national forests were set up to protect public lands.

_____ 2. Timber companies have not always used the forests wisely.

_____ 3. The only reason loggers lost jobs in the 1990s was because laws were passed to protect the spotted owl.

_____ 4. Laws passed in the 1970s helped to protect animal habitat.

_____ 5. Old-growth forests are not important animal habitat.

Discuss these questions.

1. Do you think the main use of national forests should be logging, the protection of animals and plants, hiking and camping, or something else? Explain.

2. Should the federal government be protecting our national forests? Why or why not?

A Last Look

Write about one of these topics.

1. Learn about the logging industry. What kinds of jobs are there? What do the people do?

2. Do research to learn about old-growth forests. What are they? How are they different from any other forest? Why do loggers want to cut old-growth forests? Why are they important to wildlife?

Washington

Thinking about the Picture

1. What machine is this man using?
2. Why are computers important in education and business?
3. When do you use computers? Why?

High-Tech Industries

 Washington state is a major center for technology. It is home to many software and Internet-related companies. The state is a world leader in information technology and telecommunications. Biotechnology and biomedical companies carry on research. High-tech industries are important in the state's economy.

Software is a young industry. It got its start in the Seattle area in the 1970s. Almost half of these companies have started since 1996. Since 1974, high-tech industries have grown at an explosive rate. According to an industry association, Washington has more than 6,000 software-related companies. In the year 2000, about 67,000 people were working in the industry. They produced about $30 billion in business.

One Washington company is a high-tech giant. In 1975, Bill Gates and Paul Allen started a tiny computer company in New Mexico. They named it Microsoft. Four years later they moved it to Washington, their home state. In 1980, Microsoft made a great step forward. It licensed a new operating system for personal computers (PCs). The buyer was IBM, the leading computer maker.

In 1983, Allen left Microsoft. Gates continued as head of the company. Microsoft's headquarters are in Redmond, near Seattle. It is now the largest software company in the world. In June 2002, it reported revenues of over $28 billion for the year. Nearly 25,000 people in the state worked for Microsoft.

Microsoft has been central to the growth of the high-tech industry. It has attracted other companies to the Seattle area. Its success led to many "spin-off" or "start-up" firms. Microsoft's power has also caused problems. It has had legal battles with other companies. The federal government has said that Microsoft is a monopoly.

A First Look at Vocabulary

Match each term with its meaning.

_____ **1.** computer   a. very fast

_____ **2.** software   b. income; money earned

_____ **3.** explosive   c. drawn or brought toward itself

_____ **4.** firm   d. company with unfair control over an industry

_____ **5.** revenues   e. about the law

_____ **6.** attracted   f. machine that stores and uses information

_____ **7.** legal   g. instructions that make computers work

_____ **8.** monopoly   h. company

A Second Look at Vocabulary

Choose the best answer to complete each sentence.

_____ **1.** Microsoft is the largest _____ in its industry.
    a. headquarters   b. firm   c. software

_____ **2.** You might use a _____ when you write a memo at work.
    a. biotechnology   b. monopoly   c. computer

_____ **3.** Is it _____ for a company to sell its products for less than it costs to make them?
    a. explosive   b. legal   c. economic

_____ **4.** Special _____ is used to check spelling and grammar.
    a. software   b. computer   c. system

_____ **5.** A company's success depends on how much _____ it earns.
    a. revenue   b. information   c. technology

_____ **6.** A _____ has more money and power than other companies in its industry.
    a. firm   b. monopoly   c. high-tech industry

_____ **7.** When a company has _____ growth, it may hire many new workers.
    a. reduced   b. usual   c. explosive

_____ **8.** People who want to work with computers are _____ to Microsoft.
    a. attracted   b. permitted   c. licensed

Washington

Understanding the Reading

Choose the best answer.

_____ **1.** The technology industry in Washington state
   a. has grown very rapidly since the 1970s.
   b. has become less important to Washington's economy.
   c. has more than 10,000 software-related companies.

_____ **2.** Microsoft is
   a. the world's largest software company.
   b. the world's largest biotechnology company.
   c. now moving to New Mexico.

_____ **3.** Because of Microsoft,
   a. the government has decided that software companies are monopolies.
   b. the Seattle area has lost many jobs to other parts of the country.
   c. other high-tech companies have moved to Seattle.

Reading between the Lines

Look carefully at the reading. Mark each statement _T_ for _true_ or _F_ for _false_.

_____ **1.** Almost one-half of all software companies are less than 10 years old.

_____ **2.** Bill Gates started Microsoft in Seattle in 1975.

_____ **3.** Microsoft provides about one-third of the software-related jobs in Washington.

Fact or Opinion?

Mark each statement _F_ for _fact_ or _O_ for _opinion_.

_____ **1.** Seattle became a center for technology largely because of Microsoft.

_____ **2.** Microsoft's success caused its legal problems.

_____ **3.** Licensing its operating system to IBM helped Microsoft become successful.

What Do You Think?

Discuss these questions.

1. How important is high technology in your life? How would your life be different without it?

2. Do you think technology sometimes causes problems? Explain.

3. What do you think the future of high technology is? Will the industry keep growing? Will there be more jobs or fewer jobs in 10 years? Explain why you think so.

A Last Look

Write about one of these topics.

1. What kinds of jobs are there in high technology? Do any of these jobs interest you? Which ones? Why or why not?

2. What are some of the benefits or advantages of high technology? What are some of the problems it causes? Do you think life is better or worse because of technology?

Puerto Rico

A Commonwealth

A Quick Look at this Island

Puerto Rico is 1,000 miles southeast of Florida. It lies between the Atlantic Ocean and the Caribbean Sea. Much of the island is mountainous, with lowlands along the coast. Puerto Rico is a self-governing part of the United States. Its people are U.S. citizens, but they cannot vote in presidential elections. They do not pay federal income tax. Most people speak Spanish.

Columbus landed in Puerto Rico in 1493. By 1508, the Spanish began to settle the island. The native people tried unsuccessfully to resist. Most were killed or died from European diseases. The Spanish settlers began to plant sugar cane. They brought captives from West Africa to work as slaves. Puerto Rico remained under Spanish control for about 500 years. In 1898 the United States won a war with Spain and took control of Puerto Rico.

The island has a warm, comfortable climate, which attracts tourists. In recent years, many new factories have opened on the island. Still, it has a high rate of unemployment. Millions of Puerto Ricans have come to the U.S. mainland, many to New York City.

Puerto Rico

Thinking about the Picture

1. Antonia Novello is a doctor and a public official. Why would someone choose these careers?
2. What problems do you think Dr. Novello faced?

Antonia Novello

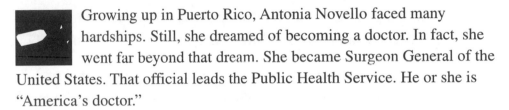 Growing up in Puerto Rico, Antonia Novello faced many hardships. Still, she dreamed of becoming a doctor. In fact, she went far beyond that dream. She became Surgeon General of the United States. That official leads the Public Health Service. He or she is "America's doctor."

Antonia Coello was born in Fajardo, Puerto Rico, in 1944. When she was 8 years old, her father died. Her mother, a teacher, had to support the family. In addition, Antonia was often in pain from an intestinal problem. At last, when she was 18, surgery corrected the condition. Antonia studied medicine at the University of Puerto Rico. In 1970, she became a doctor. The same year she married Dr. Joseph Novello, a flight surgeon in the U.S. Navy. The Novellos moved to Michigan to continue their studies. Antonia specialized in pediatrics—medical care for children.

In 1978, Dr. Novello began to work in the field of public health. She joined the U.S. Public Health Service. This federal agency tries to improve Americans' health. She dealt with issues like cigarette smoking, alcohol use by young people, and AIDS. In 1989, President George H.W. Bush chose her to be Surgeon General. She was the first woman and the first Hispanic to hold that job.

Dr. Novello was especially interested in the health of young people. As Surgeon General, she fought to limit tobacco and liquor advertising aimed at young people. She made people aware of domestic violence. She set up a vaccination program for children.

In 1993, Dr. Novello left her job as Surgeon General. She began to work with UNICEF, the United Nations Children's Fund. She worked to improve health and nutrition for women and children worldwide. In 1999, she became Commissioner of Health for New York state.

A First Look at Vocabulary

Choose the best definition for each word in bold type.

_____ 1. Which **hardships** did Antonia Novello have to deal with?
     a. illnesses   b. problems   c. jobs

_____ 2. Dr. Novello became an **official** in the federal government.
     a. high-level worker   b. voter   c. low-level worker

_____ 3. An **intestinal** illness can be very painful.
     a. of the head   b. of the muscles   c. of the body system that uses food

_____ 4. A sick child will be taken to see a doctor of **pediatrics.**
     a. children's' medicine b. nutrition   c. intestinal diseases

_____ 5. The Surgeon General **dealt with** many public health matters.
     a. became angry over b. took action on   c. thought about

_____ 6. The Surgeon General **warned** people about the dangers of smoking.
     a. told of danger   b. wrote about studies c. learned about health

_____ 7. Victims of **domestic violence** do not always talk about it.
     a. harm by a stranger b. harm by a servant   c. harm by a family member

_____ 8. Good **nutrition** will help children grow up healthy
     a. food   b. health care   c. health education

A Second Look at Vocabulary

Complete the sentences. Use the words from the first exercise.

1. If you are feeling sick to your stomach, it may be an _____ problem.

2. The police sometimes protect people from _____.

3. An _____ with the government decides how to help people.

4. Poor, sick, fatherless children have many _____ to deal with.

5. AIDS is a health problem that must be _____ by doctors around the world.

6. Even people who know about good _____ do not always eat very well.

7. Hospitals for children specialize in _____.

8. People have been _____ about the dangers of AIDS.

Puerto Rico

Understanding the Reading

Choose the best answer.

_____ **1.** As a child, Antonia Novello dealt with such hardships as
   a. loss of her father and an intestinal problem.
   b. domestic violence and cigarette smoking.
   c. use of alcohol and smoking.

_____ **2.** Novello became a doctor and
   a. worked as a teacher in Michigan.
   b. became a flight surgeon like her husband.
   c. specialized in pediatrics.

_____ **3.** When Dr. Novello became Surgeon General, she
   a. ended all liquor advertising.
   b. was the first woman and the first Hispanic to have the job.
   c. began working with the United Nations Children's Fund.

Fact or Opinion?

Mark each statement *F* for *fact* or *O* for *opinion*.

_____ **1.** Antonia Novello was the best Surgeon General ever.

_____ **2.** Dr. Novello was interested in issues relating to children.

_____ **3.** Dr. Novello believed that it was wrong to advertise cigarettes to children.

_____ **4.** Dr. Novello should have kept her job as Surgeon General.

When Did It Happen?

Write numbers to put the events in the order they happened.

_____ Novello specialized in pediatrics.

_____ Novello became a doctor.

_____ Novello became Commissioner of Health for New York.

_____ Novello became Surgeon General.

_____ Novello began working in public health.

What Do You Think?
Discuss these questions.

1. Is it important that Dr. Novello was both the first woman and the first Hispanic to be Surgeon General? Why or why not?

2. As Surgeon General, what issues did Dr. Novello work on? Do you agree that these are important health issues? Why or why not? What other issues would you include?

3. Do you think facing hardships as a child can help someone succeed later on? Why or why not?

A Last Look
Write about one of these topics.

1. What are your goals for your education? What experiences have caused you to set these goals?

2. Dr. Novello became a role model—someone that others admire—for many people. Who are your role models? How have they helped you work toward your goals?

Answer Key

Connecticut

A First Look at Vocabulary (p. 7)

1. h	3. g	5. i	7. e	9. j
2. f	4. d	6. b	8. a	10. c

A Second Look at Vocabulary (p. 7)

1. aircraft	4. fuel	7. rescue	9. flood
2. take off	5. expensive	8. sinking	10. traffic
3. rotors	6. branches		

Understanding the Reading (p. 8)

1. c   2. a   3. b

Reading between the Lines (p. 8)

1. F   2. T   3. F   4. F

Fact or Opinion? (p. 8)

1. O   2. F   3. F   4. O

Maine

A First Look at Vocabulary (p. 10)

1. b	3. a	5. b	7. c
2. a	4. c	6. a	8. b

A Second Look at Vocabulary (p. 10)

1. shell	3. trap	5. float	7. luxury
2. coastline	4. bait	6. claws	8. economy

Understanding the Reading (p. 11)

1. c   2. b   3. a   4. c   5. a

Why Did It Happen? (p. 11)

1. e   2. c   3. b   4. a   5. d

Massachusetts

A First Look at Vocabulary (p. 13)

1. e	3. a	5. i	7. c	9. b
2. g	4. f	6. d	8. j	10. h

A Second Look at Vocabulary (p. 13)

1. colonies	5. pilgrims	8. feast
2. permission	6. traditional	9. landed
3. thanksgiving	7. sailed	10. disease
4. Native Americans		

Understanding the Reading (p. 14)

1. a   2. b   3. b

Reading between the Lines (p. 14)

1. F   2. T   3. F   4. T

Why Did It Happen? (p. 14)

1. c   2. d   3. a   4. b

New Hampshire

A First Look at Vocabulary (p. 16)

1. c	3. a	5. c	7. c
2. b	4. b	6. c	8. c

A Second Look at Vocabulary (p. 16)

1. appreciate	3. inauguration	5. praised	7. emotions
2. connections	4. dropped out	6. bored	8. publishers

Understanding the Reading (p. 17)

1. b   2. c   3. a   4. c

Fact or Opinion? (p. 17)

1. O   2. F   3. F

When Did It Happen? (p. 17)

3, 4, 1, 2

Rhode Island

A First Look at Vocabulary (p. 19)

1. c	3. b	5. a	7. c
2. a	4. a	6. b	8. a

A Second Look at Vocabulary (p. 19)

1. spreading	3. synagogue	5. refused	7. worship
2. disagree	4. slavery	6. founded	8. minister

Understanding the Reading (p. 20)

1. c   2. a   3. b   4. a   5. c

When Did It Happen? (p. 20)

4, 5, 3, 1, 2, 6

Vermont

A First Look at Vocabulary (p. 22)

1. c	3. b	5. e	7. d
2. h	4. a	6. f	8. g

A Second Look at Vocabulary (p. 22)

1. c	3. c	5. b	7. a
2. a	4. c	6. c	8. a

Understanding the Reading (p. 23)

1. b   2. c   3. a   4. a   5. c

Reading between the Lines (p. 23)

1. F   2. T   3. T   4. F   5. T

Delaware

A First Look at Vocabulary (p. 26)

1. c	3. a	5. b	7. a
2. b	4. a	6. b	8. a

A Second Look at Vocabulary (p. 26)

1. pioneers	3. practical	5. settlements	7. copied
2. site	4. trunks	6. chopped	8. foundation

Understanding the Reading (p. 27)

1. c   2. b   3. b

Why Did It Happen? (p. 27)

1. b   2. d   3. a   4. c

When Did It Happen? (p. 27)

4, 2, 1, 3

District of Columbia

A First Look at Vocabulary (p. 29)

1. d	3. g	5. i	7. f	9. c
2. e	4. j	6. b	8. a	10. h

A Second Look at Vocabulary (p. 29)

1. stationery	5. federal government	8. marched
2. oath of office	6. broke out	9. contrast
3. capital	7. flee	10. ceremonies
4. Capitol		

Understanding the Reading (p. 30)

1. c   2. a   3. b

When Did It Happen? (p. 30)

2, 1, 4, 3

Reading between the Lines (p. 30)

1. T   2. F   3. T   4. F

Maryland

A First Look at Vocabulary (p. 32)

1. c   3. b   5. a   7. c
2. a   4. c   6. b   8. a

A Second Look at Vocabulary (p. 32)

1. release   4. fiercely   7. inspired
2. national anthem   5. prisoner   8. bargain
3. estate   6. patriotism

Understanding the Reading (p. 33)

1. c   2. a   3. a   4. b   5. b

Why Did It Happen? (p. 33)

1. d   2. b   3. e   4. a   5. c

New Jersey

A First Look at Vocabulary (p. 35)

1. g   3. a   5. i   7. h   9. f
2. j   4. b   6. d   8. c   10. e

A Second Look at Vocabulary (p. 35)

1. wizard   5. automatically   8. laboratory
2. telegraph   6. improvements   9. ambitious
3. patent   7. inventions   10. document
4. lightbulb

Understanding the Reading (p. 36)

1. a   2. a   3. c   4. b   5. c

Where's the Idea? (p. 36)

2, 1, 5, 4, 3

Virginia

A First Look at Vocabulary (p. 38)

1. e   3. a   5. f   7. d   9. b
2. h   4. j   6. c   8. i   10. g

A Second Look at Vocabulary (p. 38)

1. gunpowder   4. commander   7. surveyor   9. resented
2. untrained   5. elect   8. legislature   10. Tents
3. inherited   6. widow

Understanding the Reading (p. 39)

1. b   2. a   3. b   4. c   5. a

When Did It Happen? (p. 39)

3, 1, 4, 2, 5

West Virginia

A First Look at Vocabulary (p. 41)

1. c   3. b   5. b   7. a
2. b   4. c   6. c

A Second Look at Vocabulary (p. 41)

1. treason   3. issue   5. secede   7. abolitionists
2. arsenal   4. rebellion   6. hostages   8. acres

Understanding the Reading (p. 42)

1. a   2. b   3. c

Fact or Opinion? (p. 42)

1. O   2. O   3. F   4. O

When Did It Happen? (p. 42)

2, 1, 4, 3

Alabama

A First Look at Vocabulary (p. 45)

1. f   3. b   5. c   7. d
2. h   4. e   6. g   8. a

A Second Look at Vocabulary (p. 45)

1. agricultural   3. depended   5. worn out   7. blessing
2. processing   4. soil   6. pest   8. monument

Understanding the Reading (p. 46)

1. c   2. a   3. b   4. c   5. a

When Did It Happen? (p. 46)

4, 2, 5, 1, 3

Arkansas

A First Look at Vocabulary (p. 48)

1. c   3. b   5. c   7. a
2. a   4. a   6. c   8. c

A Second Look at Vocabulary (p. 48)

1. cure   3. massage   5. springs
2. elegant   4. thermal   6. eased

Understanding the Reading (p. 49)

1. b   2. c   3. a

Fact or Opinion? (p. 49)

1. F   2. F   3. O   4. F   5. O

When Did It Happen? (p. 49)

1, 4, 3, 2

Florida

A First Look at Vocabulary (p.51)

1. e   3. h   5. j   7. g   9. c
2. d   4. b   6. i   8. a   10. f

A Second Look at Vocabulary (p. 51)

1. marine   5. features   8. technology
2. perform   6. cartoon   9. Tour
3. theme park   7. old-fashioned   10. exhibit
4. character

Understanding the Reading (p. 52)

1. c   2. a   3. c

Fact or Opinion? (p. 52)

1. O   2. F   3. O   4. O

Alike or Different? (p. 52)

Name of Park	Theme	What Visitors Do
Magic Kingdom	Cartoon characters of Walt Disney	See Disney characters; visit Wild West town; see exhibits about life around the world
Universal Studios/Florida	Movies	Tour sets of movies and TV shows
Sea World	Sea creatures	Watch whales, dolphins, and seals perform; swim with dolphins; snorkel with tropical fish

Georgia

A First Look at Vocabulary (p. 54)

1. a	3. a	5. a	7. a
2. c	4. b	6. c	8. a

A Second Look at Vocabulary (p. 54)

1. amendments	4. segregated	7. nonviolent
2. civil rights	5. movement	8. bill
3. discrimination	6. protests	

Understanding the Reading (p. 55)

1. a   2. a   3. c

Reading between the Lines (p. 55)

1. F   2. T   3. T   4. T

When Did It Happen? (p. 55)

2, 3, 1,4

Kentucky

A First Look at Vocabulary (p. 57)

1. c	3. c	5. b	7. a
2. b	4. a	6. c	8. b

A Second Look at Vocabulary (p. 57)

1. oval	3. spectators	5. traditions	7. stands
2. stable	4. nickname	6. famous	8. crowd

Understanding the Reading (p. 58)

1. a   2. b   3. c   4. c   5. b

When Did It Happen? (p. 58)

3, 4, 6, 1, 2, 5

Louisiana

A First Look at Vocabulary (p. 60)

1. f	3. h	5. i	7. b	9. c
2. d	4. j	6. g	8. a	10. e

A Second Look at Vocabulary (p. 60)

1. musician	4. ancestors	7. influenced	9. parade
2. funeral	5. Jazz	8. spirituals	10. band
3. colorful	6. unique		

Understanding the Reading (p. 61)

1. a   2. b   3. a   4. c   5. b

Where's the Idea? (p. 61)

4, 2, 5, 1, 3

Mississippi

A First Look at Vocabulary (p. 63)

1. e	3. a	5. h	7. d	9. g
2. f	4. i	6. b	8. j	10. c

A Second Look at Vocabulary (p. 63)

1. prejudice	4. tired of	7. express	9. society
2. faced	5. pain	8. self-respect	10. prize
3. novel	6. abandoned		

Understanding the Reading (p. 64)

1. c   2. a   3. a   4. b

Why Did It Happen? (p. 64)

1. c   2. a   3. d   4. b

North Carolina

A First Look at Vocabulary (p. 66)

1. a	3. c	5. a	7. c
2. b	4. b	6. a	8. a

A Second Look at Vocabulary (p. 66)

1. steal	3. design	5. established	7. pilot
2. clever	4. glider	6. demonstration	8. engine

Understanding the Reading (p. 67)

1. b   2. c   3. b

Reading between the Lines (p. 67)

1. T   2. F   3. T   4. F

When Did It Happen? (p. 67)

3, 2, 4, 1

South Carolina

A First Look at Vocabulary (p. 69)

1. c	3. e	5. d	7. g	9. j
2. b	4. a	6. h	8. i	10. f

A Second Look at Vocabulary (p. 69)

1. poor	4. institute	7. support	9. agency
2. talented	5. charcoal	8. appointed	10. cane
3. scholarship	6. local		

Understanding the Reading (p. 70)

1. b   2. a   3. c   4. b

Why Did It Happen? (p. 70)

1. b   2. a   3. e   4. c   5. d

Tennessee

A First Look at Vocabulary (p. 72)

1. a	3. a	5. b	7. b
2. c	4. c	6. a	8. c

A Second Look at Vocabulary (p. 72)

1. fans	3. roots	5. elements	7. program
2. broadcast	4. fiddle	6. style	8. tunes

Understanding the Reading (p. 73)

1. b   2. b   3. a   4. c   5. a

Reading between the Lines (p. 73)

1. T   2. T   3. F   4. F   5. T

Indiana

A First Look at Vocabulary (p. 76)

1. g	3. e	5. f	7. c	9. d
2. i	4. a	6. h	8. b

A Second Look at Vocabulary (p. 76)

1. c	3. a	5. a	7. a	9. c
2. b	4. b	6. c	8. b	

Understanding the Reading (p. 77)

1. b	2. c	3. a	4. b	5. a

Reading between the Lines (p. 77)

1. T	2. T	3. F	4. T	5. F

New York

A First Look at Vocabulary (p. 79)

1. f	3. h	5. b	7. d	9. c
2. e	4. j	6. i	8. a	10. g

A Second Look at Vocabulary (p. 79)

1. opportunity	4. tablet	7. engraved	9. statue
2. platform	5. chain	8. emigrated	10. crown
3. torches	6. invitation		

Understanding the Reading (p. 80)

1. c	2. a	3. b

Fact or Opinion? (p. 80)

1. O	2. F	3. F	4. O

When Did It Happen? (p. 80)

3, 1, 2, 4

Ohio

A First Look at Vocabulary (p. 82)

1. c	3. c	5. c	7. b
2. a	4. b	6. a	8. a

A Second Look at Vocabulary (p. 82)

1. display	3. performers	5. architect	7. costumes
2. wing	4. songwriter	6. poster	8. disc jockeys

Understanding the Reading (p. 83)

1. a	2. c	3. b	4. a	5. a

Where's the Idea? (p. 83)

4, 2, 5, 1

Pennsylvania

A First Look at Vocabulary (p. 85)

1. c	3. c	5. c	7. a
2. a	4. b	6. b	8. a

A Second Look at Vocabulary (p. 85)

1. handsome	3. reunite	5. delegates	7. pursuit
2. convention	4. issue	6. inhabitants	8. claimed

Understanding the Reading (p. 86)

1. a	2. c	3. b

When Did It Happen? (p. 86)

2, 3, 1

Reading between the Lines (p. 86)

1. T	2. F	3. T	4. F

Illinois

A First Look at Vocabulary (p. 89)

1. e	3. f	5. g	7. a	9. b
2. d	4. i	6. h	8. c	

A Second Look at Vocabulary (p. 89)

1. c	3. c	5. a	7. b	9. c
2. a	4. b	6. c	8. b	

Understanding the Reading (p. 90)

1. a	2. c	3. a	4. b	5. c

Fact or Opinion? (p. 90)

1. O	2. F	3. F	4. O	5. O

Iowa

A First Look at Vocabulary (p. 92)

1. c	3. e	5. g	7. h	9. f
2. d	4. i	6. b	8. a	

A Second Look at Vocabulary (p. 92)

1. life-size	4. compete	7. lasts
2. handicrafts	5. overseas	8. harvest
3. celebrate	6. demonstration	9. fair

Understanding the Reading (p. 93)

1. c	2. a	3. b

Reading between the Lines (p. 93)

1. T	2. F	3. F	4. T

Fact or Opinion? (p. 93)

1. F	2. O	3. F	4. O

Michigan

A First Look at Vocabulary (p. 95)

1. b	3. c	5. c	7. a
2. a	4. b	6. a	8. b

A Second Look at Vocabulary (p. 95)

1. production	4. cheaper	7. Pioneers
2. afford	5. identical	
3. Metropolitan	6. foreign	

Understanding the Reading (p. 96)

1. b	2. c	3. c	4. a	5. b

When Did It Happen? (p. 96)

2, 6, 1, 5, 3, 4

Minnesota

A First Look at Vocabulary (p. 98)

1. c	3. b	5. c	7. a
2. b	4. b	6. c	8. b

A Second Look at Vocabulary (p. 98)

1. patients	4. specialty	7. clinic
2. group practice	5. Physicians	
3. surgeon	6. instruments	

Understanding the Reading (p. 99)

1. b	2. a	3. c

Fact or Opinion? (p. 99)

1. O	2. F	3. O	4. F

When Did It Happen? (p. 99)

1, 3, 4, 2

Missouri

A First Look at Vocabulary (p. 101)

1. c	3. b	5. a	7. b
2. a	4. c	6. c	8. a

A Second Look at Vocabulary (p. 101)

1. mourned	3. humor	5. ambition	7. mustache
2. pen name	4. reporter	6. published	8. steamboat

Understanding the Reading (p. 102)

1. b	2. a.	3. b	4. c

Fact or Opinion? (p. 102)

1. F   2. F   3. O

When Did It Happen? (p. 102)

3, 1, 4, 2

Wisconsin

A First Look at Vocabulary (p. 104)

1. d   3. f   5. g   7. a

2. h   4. b   6. e   8. c

A Second Look at Vocabulary (p. 104)

1. b   3. a   5. b   7. b

2. c   4. c   6. a   8. c

Understanding the Reading (p. 105)

1. a   2. c   3. b

Reading between the Lines (p. 105)

1. T   2. F   3. F   4. T

When Did It Happen? (p. 105)

4, 1, 2, 3

Colorado

A First Look at Vocabulary (p. 108)

1. a   3. b   5. a   7. b

2. b   4. c   6. c   8. a

A Second Look at Vocabulary (p. 108)

1. goggles   3. downhill   5. tourists   7. fiberglass

2. glare   4. festival   6. scenery

Understanding the Reading (p. 109)

1. b   2. a   3. c

Reading between the Lines (p. 109)

1. T   2. T   3. F

Why Did It Happen? (p. 109)

1. c   2. a   3. d   4. b

Idaho

A First Look at Vocabulary (p. 111)

1. d   3. g   5. h   7. e   9. b

2. f   4. c   6. j   8. i   10. a

A Second Look at Vocabulary (p. 111)

1. declined   4. minerals   7. ghost towns   9. gold rush

2. deposit   5. economy   8. fertilizer   10. mined

3. prospector   6. fortune

Understanding the Reading (p. 112)

1. b   2. c   3. a   4. b

Fact or Opinion? (p. 112)

1. F   2. O   3. F

When Did It Happen? (p. 112)

3, 1, 4, 2

Kansas

A First Look at Vocabulary (p. 114)

1. b   3. a   5. c   7. a

2. c   4. b   6. c   8. a

A Second Look at Vocabulary (p. 114)

1. violently   3. territory   5. homestead   7. supplies

2. raided   4. sod   6. prairie   8. illegally

Understanding the Reading (p. 115)

1. a   2. c   3. a   4. c

Why Did It Happen? (p. 115)

1. c   2. a   3. e   4. b   5. d

Montana

A First Look at Vocabulary (p. 117)

1. f   3. h   5. i   7. d   9. a

2. e   4. g   6. j   8. c   10. b

A Second Look at Vocabulary (p. 117)

1. arena   4. preserve   7. tepee   9. decorated

2. category   5. reservation   8. camp   10. saddle

3. tribal   6. reunion

Understanding the Reading (p. 118)

1. b   2. a   3. c

Fact or Opinion? (p. 118)

1. O   2. F   3. F

Where's the Idea? (p. 118)

4, 2, 1, 5, 3

Nebraska

A First Look at Vocabulary (p. 120)

1. c   3. b   5. b   7. b

2. a   4. a   6. c   8. c

A Second Look at Vocabulary (p. 120)

1. Homeless   4. programs   7. neglected

2. residents   5. hotline   8. abused

3. juvenile   6. social worker

Understanding the Reading (p. 121)

1. b   2. c   3. a

Reading between the Lines (p. 121)

1. T   2. F   3. F   4. T

When Did It Happen? (p. 121)

4, 1, 2, 3

Nevada

A First Look at Vocabulary (p. 123)

1. e   3. i   5. g   7. d   9. b

2. f   4. h   6. a   8. c

A Second Look at Vocabulary (p. 123)

1. a   3. c   5. b   7. c   9. b

2. a   4. b   6. c   8. a

Understanding the Reading (p. 124)

1. b   2. a   3. c   4. a

Reading between the Lines (p. 124)

1. T   2. F   3. F

Fact or Opinion? (p. XX)

1. O   2. F   3. O

North Dakota

A First Look at Vocabulary (p. 126)

1. g   3. a   5. h   7. d

2. f   4. b   6. e   8. c

A Second Look at Vocabulary (p. 126)

1. a   3. c   5. a   7. a

2. c   4. b   6. b   8. b

Understanding the Reading (p. 127)

1. a   2. a   3. c   4. b

Answer Key